youngWriters 2006 Poetry Competition

"I have a dream that children will one day live in a nation where they will not be judged by the color of their skin, but by the content of their character."

Martin Luther King

# I have a dream
## words to change the world

- MOTIVATE your pupils to write and appreciate poetry.
- INSPIRE them to share their hopes and dreams for the future.
- BOOST awareness of your school's creative ability.
- WORK alongside the National Curriculum or the high level National Qualification Skills.
- Supports the *Every Child Matters* - Make a Positive Contribution outcome.
- Over £7,000 of great prizes for schools and pupils.

"When I was out there I was never ever alone, there was always a team of people behind me, in mind if not in body."

Ellen MacArthur

# Inspirational Verses
## Edited by Angela Fairbrace

First published in Great Britain in 2006 by:
Young Writers
Remus House
Coltsfoot Drive
Peterborough
PE2 9JX
Telephone: 01733 890066
Website: www.youngwriters.co.uk

All Rights Reserved

© Copyright Contributors 2006

SB ISBN 1 84602 689 X

# Foreword

Imagine a teenager's brain; a fertile yet fragile expanse teeming with ideas, aspirations, questions and emotions. Imagine a classroom full of racing minds, scratching pens writing an endless stream of ideas and thoughts . . .

. . . Imagine your words in print reaching a wider audience. Imagine that maybe, just maybe, your words can make a difference. Strike a chord. Touch a life. Change the world. Imagine no more . . .

'I Have a Dream' is a series of poetry collections written by 11 to 18-year-olds from schools and colleges across the UK and overseas. Pupils were invited to send us their poems using the theme 'I Have a Dream'. Selected entries range from dreams they've experienced to childhood fantasies of stardom and wealth, through inspirational poems of their dreams for a better future and of people who have influenced and inspired their lives.

The series is a snapshot of who and what inspires, influences and enthuses young adults of today. It shows an insight into their hopes, dreams and aspirations of the future and displays how their dreams are an escape from the pressures of today's modern life. Young Writers are proud to present this anthology, which is truly inspired and sure to be an inspiration to all who read it.

# Contents

Natalie Gillingham (12)     1

**Boroughbridge High School, Boroughbridge**
| | |
|---|---|
| Jamie Bryant (14) | 2 |
| Hannah Bratley (14) | 3 |
| Tom Hussell (14) | 4 |
| Angela Walker (14) | 5 |
| Tom Parsons (14) | 6 |
| Natasha Jenner (14) | 7 |
| Zoe Curphey (13) | 8 |
| Steven Kirby (13) | 9 |
| Edward Kellett (14) | 10 |
| Zoë Ayre (14) | 11 |
| Josh Bassitt (14) | 12 |
| Callum Grant | 13 |
| Robyn Green (14) | 14 |
| David Short (14) | 15 |
| Matt Cussons (14) | 16 |
| Emily Leach & Mel Helliwell | 17 |
| Lucy Parker (14) | 18 |
| Vicky Peacock (13) | 19 |
| Matthew Barron (13) | 20 |
| Kelly Goldsmith (14) | 21 |
| Alice Gill (14) | 22 |
| Chloe Pollock (14) | 23 |
| Helena Daly (14) | 24 |
| Harry Hanson Hibbs | 25 |
| Rhys Hamilton-Evans (14) | 26 |
| Annabel Walley (14) | 27 |
| Amy Robinson (14) | 28 |
| Denise Owen | 29 |
| Taryn Mackay | 30 |
| Jessica Hartley (14) | 31 |
| Lauren Rawding & Zak Powell | 32 |
| James Cook (14) | 33 |
| George Brook (14) | 34 |
| George Welton | 35 |
| Peter Frankland (13) | 36 |

**Chapel Grange School, Allerton**
    Rabiya Razaq (11)      37

**Dunbar Grammar School, Dunbar**
    Natalie Tait (12)      38
    Lewis Richardson (13)      39
    Emma Yule (13)      40
    Robby Wilson (12)      41
    Lynsey Fletcher (12)      42
    Adam Redpath (13)      43
    Olivia Dewar (12)      44
    Douglas McClintick (12)      46
    Gayle Forsyth (12)      48
    Ailsa Fineron (12)      49
    Holly Nicholson (13)      50
    Nicholas Denholm (12)      51
    Danny Munroe (12)      52
    Julie Huggan (13)      54
    Katharine Duguid (12)      55

**Gourock High School, Gourock**
    Debbie Moore (13)      56
    Peter Nimmo (14)      57
    Andrew Clark (13)      58

**Porthcawl Comprehensive School, Porthcawl**
    Robyn Govier      59
    Corey Bridgeman (13)      60
    Luke Nicholas (12)      61
    Nick Gillingham (12)      62
    Courtney Sims (12)      63
    Nicole Robbins (12)      64
    Bethanie Denyer (12)      65
    Owain Morgan (13)      66
    Jade Wallis (13)      67
    Rhys Thomas (13)      68
    James Harris (13)      69
    Jade Bickerstaff (13)      70
    Georgina Evans (11)      71
    Georgina Dorr (11)      72

| | |
|---|---|
| Cheryl McAndrew  (12) | 73 |
| Alex Nia Howells  (11) | 74 |
| Sophie Howe  (11) | 75 |
| Rachel Tayler  (12) | 76 |
| Emma Bold  (13) | 77 |
| Charlotte Wardman  (13) | 78 |
| Rebecca Thomas  (13) | 79 |
| Thomas Leach  (13) | 80 |
| Roisin Evans  (11) | 81 |
| Kathryn Allen  (12) | 82 |
| Hannah Gibbins  (13) | 83 |
| Katrina Davies  (12) | 84 |
| Rebecca Jones  (13) | 85 |
| Elliott Jenkins  (12) | 86 |
| Ashleigh Furness  (13) | 87 |
| Josh Prescott  (13) | 88 |
| Matthew Evans  (13) | 89 |
| Angharad Davies  (12) | 90 |
| Nia Challenger  (12) | 91 |
| Abigail Weale  (13) | 92 |
| Sam Williams  (13) | 93 |
| Emma Hill  (13) | 94 |
| Amy Rhys  (12) | 95 |
| Jacob Chappell  (13) | 96 |
| Kelly Ann Dyde  (13) | 97 |
| Josie Loye  (12) | 98 |
| Jak Kent  (13) | 99 |
| Lewis Jones  (12) | 100 |
| Samantha Hopkins  (12) | 101 |
| Andrew McQueen  (12) | 102 |
| Imogen Lewis-Davidson  (13) | 103 |
| Lizzie Crocker  (13) | 104 |
| Chelsea Gatter  (12) | 105 |
| Leah Richards  (11) | 106 |
| Drew Richards  (12) | 107 |
| Lauren Jones  (12) | 108 |
| Connor Moody  (11) | 109 |
| Charlotte Tasker  (11) | 110 |
| Rebecca Maddern  (11) | 111 |
| Nathan Gillingham  (13) | 112 |
| Shelley Heanue  (12) | 113 |
| Tahlia Platts  (13) | 114 |

| | |
|---|---|
| Roberto Rossini  (12) | 115 |
| Alice Power  (13) | 116 |
| Hannah Brown  (12) | 117 |
| Ferdinand Ball  (12) | 118 |
| Jonathan Phillips  (13) | 119 |
| Rebecca Bates  (12) | 120 |
| Rachel Ellis  (12) | 121 |

**Rye St Anthony School, Headington**

| | |
|---|---|
| Alice Jenkins  (13) | 122 |
| Eleanor Judges  (12) | 123 |
| Natasha Turner  (15) | 124 |
| Natalie Balchin  (17) | 125 |

**St Francis Xavier School, Richmond**

| | |
|---|---|
| April Green  (11) | 126 |
| Devon Lowe  (12) | 127 |
| Hayley Gill  (12) | 128 |
| Lucy Bartram  (12) | 129 |
| Joe Mingay  (12) | 130 |
| Rachael Ditchburn  (12) | 131 |
| Danielle Falconer  (12) | 132 |
| Lauren Perry  (11) | 133 |
| Natascha Carne  (11) | 134 |
| Victoria Carter  (12) | 135 |
| Hannah Hill  (12) | 136 |
| Jemma Elliott  (13) | 137 |
| Jennifer Barker  (13) | 138 |
| Anna Regan  (13) | 139 |
| Sophie Carter  (13) | 140 |
| Frances Finn  (13) | 141 |
| William Alderson  (13) | 142 |
| Danielle Cawood  (13) | 143 |
| Hannah Robinson  (13) | 144 |
| Paige Howard  (12) | 145 |
| Lilly McNabb  (13) | 146 |
| Sam Thompson  (13) | 147 |
| Ryan Bishop  (13) | 148 |
| Sophie Meehan  (12) | 149 |
| Rebekah Slinger  (12) | 150 |
| Stephanie Shepherd  (12) | 151 |

| | |
|---|---|
| Elizabeth Roe  (12) | 152 |
| Kaitha Pennell  (12) | 153 |
| Ben Wilbor & Thomas Armstrong  (12) | 154 |
| Matthew Atkins  (12) | 155 |
| James Walker  (12) | 156 |
| Sophie Whittaker  (12) | 157 |
| Emma Everitt & Chelsea Jones  (13) | 158 |
| Emma Snodgrass & Louise Pearson  (13) | 159 |
| James Simpson  (13) | 160 |
| Kate Renolds-Scott  (13) | 161 |
| Rhianna McCowan  (13) | 162 |
| Louise Davies  (13) | 163 |
| Abbie Taylor  (14) | 164 |
| Kerry-Ann Gray  (14) | 165 |
| Rachael Baty  (14) | 166 |
| Katie Cunningham  (14) | 167 |
| Katie Brown  (14) | 168 |
| Gareth Handley  (12) | 169 |

**St Mary Redcliffe & Temple CE School, Bristol**

| | |
|---|---|
| Paul Dury  (12) | 170 |
| Gareth Bromley  (12) | 171 |
| Jessica Warrey  (12) | 172 |
| Amy Dutch  (12) | 173 |
| Chad Edwards  (13) | 174 |

# The Poems

## I Have A Dream

I have a dream that one day
I will change the world,
I will change all bad things into good
I have a dream that one day little black boys and girls join hands
with little white boys and girls,
I have a dream today!

I have a dream that everyone should be treated the same,
No one should be judged by the colour of their skin,
But by who they are.
I have a dream today!

I have a dream that everyone will be happy,
Everyone will smile and laugh,
Everyone will have fun and play games,
Why must everyone fight?
Why does everyone argue?
Why is there death in the world?
I have a dream,
I have a dream today.

**Natalie Gillingham (12)**

## I Have A Dream

That I will walk out with the England cricket team,
Play for them, that's my dream,
To play at Lords and score a hundred,
It's something that I have always wondered,
You never know, it could come true,
I still have 20 years or two.

**Jamie Bryant (14)**
**Boroughbridge High School, Boroughbridge**

## Water

I feel sorry for the people living in Third World countries,
Water is scarce or there is none at all,
Imagine . . .

Every litre of it would have to be carefully watched
And planned as to how you would use it,
In rich countries like America and England,
Water is plentiful and we have it in our homes straight from the taps,

So next time you are cleaning your teeth or washing up,
Just remember that others are less fortunate than you,
So do not waste water, use it sparingly.

**Hannah Bratley (14)**
**Boroughbridge High School, Boroughbridge**

# I Have A Dream

I have a dream of planets and stars
That one day we will reach
Until that time I'll still ponder and dream
On a beach with its moonlight beam

Imagine living on the moon
That *will* happen soon
We'll have no air to breathe
Oh no, we'll have to leave.

**Tom Hussell (14)**
**Boroughbridge High School, Boroughbridge**

# I Have A Dream

A thousand times I stop in places, to think about the world,
to look upon a million faces,
that never can be heard.

I stop in several different places, though they all look the same,
the people there behind those faces,
never ask my name.

I walk along a path of tears, that only I can see,
reflections of the ones I lost,
smiling back at me.

I have already seen all of these places, in a past dream,
but nothing feels right anymore,
it's more difficult than it seems.

I try to choose another path, to leave the lost behind,
but even as I turn away,
it's them I always find.

Those devilish eyes that watch down on me, but they never
                                                    can be seen,
the path is very dark now,
no one will hear me scream.

I want to forget these memories, as some I don't want to see,
the man who killed my parents,
just smiling, looking at me.

When I flee the faces too, I see the one I love,
his brown eyes that blind my heart,
his soul fluttering like a dove.

My memories of the world, the world I see today,
my dreams are torn apart,
the memories that will haunt me every day.

So if the world was a happy place, a happy place to be,
no poverty, murders and bad things in life,
then I'll jump with glee.

**Angela Walker (14)**
**Boroughbridge High School, Boroughbridge**

## A Typical Day Of Struggle

And so once again
I woke from my bed
And stared out my bedroom window,
Stared at the endless desert of hunger and thirst and struggle.
I saw my parents dig for water,
Hunt for food and fight the incredible heat.
I dig deep into my own head
And I see the future.
My family and I were not in it.
My education is over,
My family cannot pay my school.
My family becomes ill.
It seems that nothing can help me escape from this place.
Will nobody help us?

Then I wake from my nightmare,
I'm back in my normal bedroom.
Back to a life that is good.
Water and food is plenty in our house.
But I realise, my nightmare is actually reality,
People die from poverty
And does anybody care?
I have a dream.
A dream of no more poverty.
A dream I so hope will one day come true.

**Tom Parsons (14)**
**Boroughbridge High School, Boroughbridge**

## I Have A Dream

Bills, bills
More and more bills
I'm frustrated, it's frustrating
I need some pills!

Fees, fees
It's doctor's fees
Money, money
I'm losing money!

Why, why are there so many bills?
Electricity and the water supply
Why oh why, I need to cry!

Working and working
To keep my home
My clothes and food
I need a home!

Busy, busy
My life is so packed
Cooking, cleaning and working
Oh damn, now I'm sacked!

**Natasha Jenner (14)**
**Boroughbridge High School, Boroughbridge**

# I Have A Dream

I have two main goals in life
And can only succeed in one way
And that is by working hard to achieve it.

This dream is to prevent pollution and drugs
For I feel that other things in life can wait for me.

This may seem like a big mission to others,
But, they can also succeed if they never give up.
If you do all the things you can
You can make a big difference in life.

Others do join me, so you can too
By having this dream . . .
And trying to make it come true.

**Zoe Curphey (13)**
**Boroughbridge High School, Boroughbridge**

## I Have A Dream

Water, water all around
But there are places where it can't be found

I have a dream that all countries will have clean water

There is food to be made in Crete
But some countries struggle to get food to eat

I have a dream that all countries will have food

There are doctors around waiting for a call to survive
But in some countries they're all busy struggling to keep people alive

I have a dream that all countries will have free healthcare when
                                                                               they need it.

**Steven Kirby (13)**
**Boroughbridge High School, Boroughbridge**

## Change The World

To change the world we must go the right way
Make things better day by day.
Open your ears, hear people's fears,
Open your eyes, see people cry.
Many people are suffering,
They can't get out, let's tell the world, let's shout it out.
People screaming about the past,
Not dreaming for the future.
People lie, people cry, people die,
People say what can I do?
But everyone can help, even you.

**Edward Kellett (14)**
**Boroughbridge High School, Boroughbridge**

# I Would Make The Sun Shine Every Day . . .

One morning,
You might wake up and not see any point anymore,
But if the sun is shining through your window on that day,
You might realise that's one good reason to get out of bed.

One afternoon,
You could be at the end of your tether,
But if the sun is shining down on you,
You might be able to hold on that little longer.

One day,
Someone might tell you, you've got no chance of achieving what you want,
But if that big golden star is peeping through the clouds,
You might feel a little more determined.

One evening,
You might dread the thought of another day,
But if you knew it was going to be sunny tomorrow,
You might still have some hope left inside.

If the sun did shine every day,
It might make that day a little more special.

**Zoë Ayre (14)**
**Boroughbridge High School, Boroughbridge**

## Bush Makes Mistake

Here is my poem for you to read,
World peace is what we need.
Violence and fighting happens every day,
Women and children never have a say.
Soldiers fighting in Iraq,
These soldiers need to come back.
President Bush made a mistake,
He never thought to hesitate.
America went to war for oil
And England had to be loyal.
Hundreds of men have died,
So many wives have cried.
Many wars are fought for cash,
Young men die in a flash.
The marines go in and kill the enemy,
But really they are the enemy,
Causing so much death,
Not leaving one single breath.
We need to stop all wars,
President Bush is the biggest cause.

**Josh Bassitt (14)**
**Boroughbridge High School, Boroughbridge**

## Good Like Bluebell Wood

To make the world good
Like Bluebell Wood,
I think we should do these things.

Don't go to Iraq,
Where the rat-a-tat-tat,
Is the bell of death for a few.

Turn to solar power
And praise Eisenhower,
Before Mr Bush rules the world.

Do good deeds
And don't spray weeds,
So we can keep the flowers.

To make the world good
Like Bluebell Wood,
We'd better do these things.

**Callum Grant**
**Boroughbridge High School, Boroughbridge**

## Water

Why do we have baths not showers
When we know some people have nothing?
Why do we take water for granted?
We abuse it in every way,
When a drip of water means life,
People go to sleep on an empty stomach,
Not being able to afford
The smallest bit of water.

Huge companies taking over water supplies,
Making massive profits,
Increasing inequality across the world,
Feeding the world's greed,
Meeting the world's demands.

**Robyn Green (14)**
**Boroughbridge High School, Boroughbridge**

## Open Your Eyes

Open your eyes, just open your eyes
Look at the slavery, look at the poverty

Stop! Just stop! I hear you cry
Life will get better
It always does
We will all see, we will all see

All we need to do is spread your love
And affection to the world around

So jump off your bikes and stop digging your jumps
And open your eyes, just open your eyes
Stop filling your car up
And open your eyes, just open your eyes

Don't you see!
Just open your eyes!

**David Short (14)**
**Boroughbridge High School, Boroughbridge**

## Stop The Killing, Start The Healing

Why are there wars? What is won by wars?
When they could think it through
*Peace*
*Peace*
*Peace*
Why is there war in the world? There is no need to fight each other!
Let's stop the killing and start the healing
Accept people for who they are
There's no difference, they are who they are
In the war it's just a normal person on the floor
A bullet in his head and a bullet in his leg
He will lie and die
While we sigh and try
To make a difference.

**Matt Cussons (14)**
**Boroughbridge High School, Boroughbridge**

## I Have A Dream . . .

I have a dream that fear and horror turn to happiness
Hate turns to love
Dreams turn to reality
Then bullying turns to friendship.

I have a dream that the bad people turn to good
Everyone does their deed to help the world
I have a dream war turns to agreement
Poverty turns to wealth.

I have a dream that bad luck turns to good
Failing turns to achievement
Death turns to new life
Illness turns to health

I have a dream that everybody can be treated equally
Tears turn to smiles
Darkness turns to light
So never give up and do your deed to inspire the world.

**Emily Leach & Mel Helliwell**
**Boroughbridge High School, Boroughbridge**

## I Have A Dream To Change The World To A Better Place For All!

I dream of the world a better place

H oping all the wars would end
A ll nations to live in peace
V iolence to cease around the globe
E veryone living a peaceful life

A ll countries have food enough for all

D on't waste the time you have
R emember once it has gone you don't get it back
E veryone has a right to a view
A ll are not the same as you
M ake an effort to get on with all.

**Lucy Parker (14)**
**Boroughbridge High School, Boroughbridge**

## I Have A Dream To Change The World

I have a dream to change this world.
To make it a better place for us to live for young ones to grow up in.
To make this world better we don't want horrible things to happen like
Fights, wars and slavery.
We want these things to stop this minute.
I have a dream to change the world.
So every single one of us is equal.
I have a dream to change the world,
So that it's peaceful and calm with no shouting or falling outs.
I have a dream to change the world,
So that everyone has a smile upon their face,
With happiness and enjoyment.

**Vicky Peacock (13)**
**Boroughbridge High School, Boroughbridge**

## Change The World!

Just think of the world!

Bad things are happening every day,
Most of you know that, you just hide it away.
You think there is nothing you can do,
But there's really a lot just one can do too.

Just think of the world we have today
And think of a way to make the bad things go away.
Just think of the world because if you do not,
People will starve and die on the spot.

**Matthew Barron (13)**
**Boroughbridge High School, Boroughbridge**

## I Have A Dream

I have a dream to change the world
Make the pain stop
That all the people give out
Change the way of life

I have a dream
To stop the slavery
To end the cruelty
To end the war
End all the fights

I have a dream
For people to be equal
To not let people feel unwanted
So let people feel wanted.

**Kelly Goldsmith (14)**
**Boroughbridge High School, Boroughbridge**

## I Had A Dream That Everyone Were Friends!

I had a dream that every little girl and every little boy were friends,
They would all be friends and play in the park.
Their parents wouldn't mind where they would be,
They could go out and go to the sports centre!

Children could all go to the same school,
They could all laugh and play in the school pool.
They could all have a good laugh and try and work hard,
Then they would get good grades and in the end they
                                        wouldn't get barred!

When they are adults they would have partners and children,
They could celebrate their birthday and have fun together.
They could go on family days out to the zoo and theme parks,
But not every family and friends turn out like that!

**Alice Gill (14)**
**Boroughbridge High School, Boroughbridge**

# What Has Our World Come To Today?

What is out there in our world today?
Wars, AIDS and suffering, no way!

We open our eyes to wars and death
And cope with everyday lives full of stress
The days get shorter
As some grow old
Pressures of this day are far worse, so I'm told

Terrorism, poverty and disease
Are part of today's controversies
Friendship, health and equal rights
Could end all these unwanted fights

To some, money is everything
What about the people who are suffering?
They need it most
But millionaires don't share, just boast

What is out there in our world today?
War, AIDS and suffering, no way!

As my grandad would say
What a shame life wasn't the same as in his day
And if he had his way
Life would be so much better off today.

**Chloe Pollock (14)**
**Boroughbridge High School, Boroughbridge**

## Equal Rights

I have a dream
Where there is a theme
Of both darkness and light
Where we all have equal rights

And whether you are happy or sad
Calm or mad
You will be treated the same as everyone else
And whether your name's Harry or Tom
No matter where you are from
You will be treated the same as everyone else
And whether you like punk or pop
Like to skate or shop
You will be treated the same as everyone else

In my dream
There is a theme
Of both darkness and light
Where we all have equal rights.

**Helena Daly (14)**
**Boroughbridge High School, Boroughbridge**

## Freedom For All

Halls of justice painted green,
Take *your* money as *they* please,
Fall to your knees,
The hammer of power crushes *you,*
They leave their trademark on you,
Devour,

Power factories trick the public eye,
Secrets are all the lies,
Make their negative wrongs
Into very negative rights,

*You'll* satisfy their appetites
And when they are done,
They'll go at *your* expense,
Leaving you no way to express,
Leaving all who cower,
Leaving them all behind,

The ultimate in vanity,
Exploiting their supremacy,
Lady Justice herself has been raped,
Their money tips her scales again,
Your silence for your confidence,
They keep *you* where they must,
Freedom no longer frees *you.*

**Harry Hanson Hibbs**
**Boroughbridge High School, Boroughbridge**

## A War That Was Not Their Own

In a war that was not their own
No one wanted them to leave home
Hundreds dead, a few more dying
Think of the women and children crying

Thousands of protesters trying
To stop the pain and lying
A child asks, 'Why
Did Daddy have to die?'

In a country with a strange name
So small but with so much fame
The war here has finished
Pleasing all those who wished

But the soldiers are still coming home
In a box packed with foam
Blood over their once young eyes
They won't get a chance to ask, 'Why?'

**Rhys Hamilton-Evans (14)**
**Boroughbridge High School, Boroughbridge**

## One Day

One day the world could be a better place,
All could be equal,
All could have the same,
One day.

One day people could be perfect,
There could be no need for war, prisons or strife
Life could be a wonderful thing,
One day.

That one day,
There could be no disgrace,
Everyone could live together,
In tune, as one, in harmony.
One day.

One day there could be no racism,
No poverty, no innocent children,
Lying starving at our feet.
One day.

One day *must* happen,
One day *must* come,
For if we give up,
The world will have won.

Let's promise ourselves.
One day.

**Annabel Walley (14)**
**Boroughbridge High School, Boroughbridge**

## Front Page Headlines No One Listens To

'Thousands dead'
'Our sewage seas'
'A million lives claimed by disease'
'10 more cancers'
'No more chances'
'We're all angry - we want answers!'
'No more rainforest!'
'No fresh air'
'Poverty on the increase'
'Does anyone care?'
God, are *You* still reading our front pages?

**Amy Robinson (14)**
**Boroughbridge High School, Boroughbridge**

## Stars In The Night Sky

I have a dream
And in my dream hope gleams
Like stars in the midnight sky
The dreams of children swoop and fly
They go so far they cannot be seen
Over the moon past the furthest star.

Children living in poverty know nothing of hope
Shining in the midnight sky
Nobody knows how they cope
Although they try to be happy
It's plain to see with their bones showing
And skin like ice cream cones
Their sunken faces etched with hunger
They know they are in danger of starving
Though some are still thriving
This is thanks to the lights in the darkness
The few helpful souls willing to clean and serve bowls
Of life giving food
To those of sorrowful mood
They are lost in the darkness never to be bright
Until we fight
To help those souls regain their light
Forever to shine in the midnight sky.

**Denise Owen**
**Boroughbridge High School, Boroughbridge**

# Thinking What Is

Think what is;
Pollution, litter, dirt.
Think what could be;
Fresh air and a clean world.

Think what is;
Crime, murder and rape.
Think what could be;
Long lives, in harmony.

Think what is;
Poverty, starvation.
Think what could be;
No one suffering from dehydration.

Which world would you rather think of?
Which world would you rather live in?
What should be done for this world?
What could be done for this world?

Don't *think* what the world is now, *do* what you want it to be.

**Taryn Mackay**
**Boroughbridge High School, Boroughbridge**

## The World Keeps Trippin'

What we have here is failure, charged guilty,
I don't want this world to be dirty and filthy,
I think of things that only dreams are made of,
Not greed and war exchanging quicker than a cough.

War Vs peace is the same old game,
So many wars have happened I can't remember their name,
They say 'the grass is always greener on the other side',
But people are scared of the truth so they hide.

Weapons, murder and war, also blood,
All these words should be kicked out for good,
No one seems to put a stop to these wars,
Whose problem is it? Hers? His? Mine or yours?

We should fight our battle to stamp out the terror and fear,
So no one would cry, no one would shed a single tear,
I don't like this any more than you men,
These things can't be solved with a bit of paper and pen.

Look at the hate we have created,
There is no love, it's just tainted,
I want to stop this today like you fellow brothers,
It's my dream for this generation as it was for your fathers and mothers.

**Jessica Hartley (14)**
**Boroughbridge High School, Boroughbridge**

## If I Could Change The World . . .

When the world was created did we know that in a matter of
time it would be destroyed?
It was our fate that we could not avoid . . .
Pollution, disaster and fighting hereafter
Memories of a peaceful world have begun to fade
People living off the world's given aid

Now it's disappearing and we're in fear
People starving and wasting their tears
The heat is increasing
The ice caps are decreasing
And soon there will be no more
All the world's water beginning to pour

In a few years' time will we still be here?
A disastrous world will soon be near
Can we stop this destructive vision
And is it us to make this big decision?
We will be here in a couple of years
Who knows what the future holds my dear.

**Lauren Rawding & Zak Powell**
Boroughbridge High School, Boroughbridge

## I Have A Dream

Would you like a perfect world
Where world peace would unfold?

Would you like a perfect week
Where nobody gets called a geek?

Would you like a perfect day
Where you could get into bed to lay?

Now the world always fears
Everyone bursting into tears

All of Africa dying of starvation
Always looking for some kind of salvation

Wars always killing innocent people
There's no safety anymore in the church's steeple.

**James Cook (14)**
**Boroughbridge High School, Boroughbridge**

## Poverty

Children starving because of money
Can't even afford a pot of honey.

Haven't got enough money to pay
The outcome's starting to look grey.

Help to cancel Third World debt
That would be a worthwhile bet.

Disease and AIDS spreading fast
Is the world going to last?

The water is as good as gone
Sitting on a ticking bomb

The western world sucking them dry
Leaving them to shrivel and die.

**George Brook (14)**
**Boroughbridge High School, Boroughbridge**

## One Vision

I tried to change the world today
I was often stuck for words to say
People dying all over the world
Helpless people who can't be heard
Slavery, rape, murder too
All committed by people like you.

I tried to change the world today
There are few words that I can say
So let's make this world a better place
Let's not throw it back in their face
There are so many things that we can do
So let's make it better for them not you!

**George Welton**
**Boroughbridge High School, Boroughbridge**

## Why?

Why is water see-through?
Why is water soft?
How does water clean us?
How does water feed us?

We give the water to the dog
Why do we throw our water away like a bag of rubbish?

Why do we use the water in the garden?
Why do we leave the tap running?
Why do we wash our cars?

How come we have no money?
How come we have no water to drink?
How come they built a Coca-Cola factory here?
Please, please give us some water.

**Peter Frankland (13)**
**Boroughbridge High School, Boroughbridge**

## I Have A Dream

I feel sad

H ungry people
A re starving
V ery poor people
E verybody

A ll the time

D eserving
R ights
E qually
A stonishingly cruel
M oney madness.

**Rabiya Razaq (11)**
**Chapel Grange School, Allerton**

## Words To Change The World

Artists singing
About people killing
No more fighting
It's not exciting
Children crying
Parents lying
Is there any help around?

Bombs falling
Leaders calling
Searching for attention
More nuclear bombs created
Leads to the inventors being hated
Listen to your heart
Is this the right thing to do?

Do you ever think
We could become extinct?
If all the bombs and war vanished
Would the chaos all be gone?
If leaders finished fighting
Would the grass be much greener on the other side
Leading to a more cheerful dawn?

**Natalie Tait (12)**
**Dunbar Grammar School, Dunbar**

## What's Happening?

The world is slowly heating up,
The water level is rising
And people have started terrorising,
Many babies are now crying,
All because the world is heating up.

The ice caps are slowly melting,
Countries have started fighting,
Can't we just work together?
At least until the ice caps stop melting.

Powerful trucks are causing pollution,
The ozone is slowly disappearing,
The water level is also rising,
Our world must be coming to an end
And the powerful trucks are helping.

There is even a global terror threat,
They think the world is their pet,
Isn't it time to do something?
Cars exploding, people are dying,
All because of the global terror threat.

**Lewis Richardson (13)**
**Dunbar Grammar School, Dunbar**

## Racism

Why must they stop and stare?
Do they wonder?
Do they care
About the feelings I have inside
About the hurting I try to hide?

Words slice like knives into my heart,
Once said never forgotten.
Words to make my world fall apart,
The pathway to a brighter future closes;
I am the thorn in a bunch of red roses.

An angering cloud will forever hang above me,
With no trace of sunlight anymore.
How did I take so long to see?
I am wanted no more.
I wasn't wanted any more . . .

**Emma Yule (13)**
Dunbar Grammar School, Dunbar

# Big Issue

Car fumes are a wetsuit,
Heating up our planet,
The cities are ant hills,
Each one doing their part
To bring down the predator,
Who is defenceless and alone.

The pollution we humans produce,
Is a rising smoke,
Slowly suffocating Earth,
Our planet is a victim,
A victim of bullying
Who is defenceless and alone.

Our species today is selfish,
We do not consider the animals,
Or our children or the future,
Global warming is as bad as torture,
We're slowly murdering our planet,
Who is defenceless and alone.

**Robby Wilson (12)**
**Dunbar Grammar School, Dunbar**

## Animal Cruelty

Animal cruelty?
Animal abuse?
Why do we do it?
What is the use?

Do they realise
What they're doing is wrong?
Do they wonder?
Do they care?

When an animal sits and waits,
For the master they trust,
Waiting and waiting,
Waiting for someone who might never come.

They can't tell,
If they've done something wrong.
They can't see,
Why their master has abandoned them.

An animal can't say what's wrong,
Can't tell anyone what's the matter.
They have to fight alone,
Fighting a silent war!

**Lynsey Fletcher (12)**
**Dunbar Grammar School, Dunbar**

## World Issues

We all must bring racism to an end
A message to all I long to send
The colours of the world
All join as one
For the Lord is our shepherd
And we are His sons
Christ made mankind in the image of Him
So please let us all, end racism

Pollution so horrible I cannot tell
Pollution makes the world smell
For a solution to stop pollution
We must minimise
The people around the world should open their eyes
Don't wait for it to get to its worst
The ozone is about to burst

There have been moments in history
That have left us shocked to the core
Attacks on innocent people
Deaths through senseless war
This world has been suffering
As humans, we all bleed
As humans we all belong here
No matter what race or creed

Their skin soaks up the heat
Leaving it as black as the midnight sky
Their eyes wide, white, pleading
Begging to the passer-by
They litter the street
Half-naked bodies
Their feet are red raw
Searching for a way out
A way out of the circle of poverty.

**Adam Redpath (13)**
Dunbar Grammar School, Dunbar

## Train Bombings

In the train, bumping along,
Lots of passengers I'm among.
Travelling on the underground train,
Everything around me looks dull and plain.
But that was all about to change,
Because someone evil had arranged . . .

A bomb was going to set
And these bad people were going to let,
All these innocent people suffer,
Someone's uncle, someone's mother.
So it was the plan,
A bomb in a rucksack, on a man.

Back on the train,
Everything plain,
Until that massive explosion came
And I wish it were just a game.
Lots of screams, lots of panic,
Everything around me had gone manic.

Shattered glass from the door,
Stared at me from the floor.
I bent down and started to crawl,
Images in my head were just awful.
Blood trickling down my face,
Injured people lay in every place.

I finally found a big enough space,
To get out of this manic place,
So I squeezed my scratched body through,
Which gave me bruises deep shades of blue,
But I was glad to get out of there
And breathe in a calmer air.

A man in yellow coat found me
And took a look at my worst injury,
Broken glass stuck in my hips,
But no words left my lips.
Too many thoughts flying through my head,
Thinking about the people that were dead.

It took a while to recover,
I stayed at home with my mother.
Then one day I began to realise,
The experience had made me a bit more wise.
That I was lucky to have my life,
My children and my wife.

Many people lost loved ones that day,
A journey, I thought, would be plain.
But later did I discover,
It had changed my life forever.
So my heart goes out to those souls,
Who now have to move on with their lives and achieve new goals.

**Olivia Dewar (12)**
**Dunbar Grammar School, Dunbar**

## The World's Playground

In the playground there's the USA,
A fat and spoilt, rich bully,
There's also Britain and Canada,
Who help the USA truly.

There are the other children,
Who are helpful, friendly, loyal and true,
Some of which the USA bullies,
For their stuff of value.

The equivalent of USA's money,
is the number of hairs on his head,
If he gave away some of that money,
Then not so many others would be dead.

The nits on USA's head,
Are the numbers of his armies,
Sucking blood from everyone,
Careless and happy and barmy.

The grease and sweat pouring out of USA's body,
Represents USA's oil,
While they have loads and loads,
Others are left in turmoil.

The bacteria crawling over USA's skin,
Are the people the USA adore,
Some are good and some are bad,
But either way he's getting more and more.

USA's pockets are flowing with money,
Which are like its nuclear missiles,
When one of them is launched,
It puts another country in exile.

There's lots of shoe marks on the playground,
Where USA's stamped his boots,
It's a mark of his authority
And stamps wherever it suits.

That is the world's playground,
Where all the countries go out to play,
There's Britain, Canada and the others,
But biggest of all is the USA.

Now maybe you'll remember this,
When USA go to war,
Hurting all the little countries,
When most were already poor.

**Douglas McClintick (12)**
**Dunbar Grammar School, Dunbar**

# The World

What has happened to the world?
Guns blazing
Children gazing
All alone in a corner
People screaming
Others dreaming
Bang and the world is gone

Animals dying all around!
Lions roaring
Blood pouring
Dead animals on the ground
Broken bones
Sharp cones
Can anyone help us?

**Gayle Forsyth (12)**
**Dunbar Grammar School, Dunbar**

## Bush

'I do believe that mankind and fish can coexist peacefully.'
The thrilling words,
They charm and deceive.

From the mouth of a rock,
They pour and pour.
Until America,
Is no more.

The oil,
That greasy gold.

It's killing us, but do we care?

'No,' says the rock.

And torture,
Of innocents.
Who scream out guilty lies,
Stop using it? It doesn't work!

'No,' says the rock.

Iraq,
The killing.
The deaths of those we love,

'Yes,' says the rock.

**Ailsa Fineron (12)**
**Dunbar Grammar School, Dunbar**

## Let's Begin!

When this world was made,
It was so neat and clean.
The ponds and rivers were a sight to be seen,
But now it's a struggle to keep things clean.

Pollution needs to be minimised,
The people around the world should open their eyes.
Don't wait until it comes to the worst,
The ozone layer is about to burst!

The sea levels rising like a bath overflowing,
Diseases are spreading like a leaking pen.
Pollution is like a blanket of death,
Oil spillages are easily spread!

If you believe in what I say,
Then you'll remember this poem each and every day,
Because now the world is falling apart,
We need to begin, to help, to start!

**Holly Nicholson (13)**
**Dunbar Grammar School, Dunbar**

## Do You Realise?

Do you realise we're destroying our planet
Most of us don't even care about
While some suicide bombers
Are destroying people's futures

George Bush and Tony Blair
Don't even seem to care
About their countries destroying the planet
They have no clear plan to solve it
All of the burning fuels
Build up the molecules
That destroy the ozone layer
We're all like a losing poker player
Losing all our belongings

Aren't we trying to stop terrorists
But some still live here in the UK
Why do they want to make us pay?
What have we done, what is it?
All we do doesn't change a bit
The CIA and the FBI can't fish them out
The terrorists are still out and about
All of these people pass away
Count them up and there will be one for every day

Aren't religions about peace?
But all their fighting will never cease
Why do they fight over any random city?
Why do the fighters have no pity
On their so called enemies?
Why don't they join up their ceremonies
Like one big happy family
And live in harmony?
But they won't, oh no

Lord, all of this is happening
And all our seas are lapping
Please come and help us
Come and help us
So we will live in peace and harmony.

**Nicholas Denholm (12)**
**Dunbar Grammar School, Dunbar**

# The World

The world is a playground, in a way
Where all the countries go out to play.
There's Brazil, the football kings
And Italy, whose operas sing.
But the lord of the playground,
Is Uncle Sam, the US of A.

The USA in his steel-capped boots,
With his soldier's nits, right down to his roots.
While all his teeth flash,
His boots go and smash,
All that stand in his way,
Uncle Sam, The US of A.

There are many hairs on his greasy head,
All in all they equal his money, or so it is said,
But some say there is more,
Locked in an overseas store.
He is certainly the richest of all,
Uncle Sam, the US of A.

And all the bacteria crawling over his skin
Equal his population, though not all are his kin.
Thousands, millions,
Maybe even billions,
Are all the people,
Of Uncle Sam, the US of A.

Canada and the UK are his cronies
Though he calls them his best buddies
So say the politicians
While they send them on their missions
For the playground king,
Uncle Sam, the US of A.

And maybe it is true, that he bullies true,
Forcing them to give him things of value,
When nits on Iraqi soil
Look after all the oil,
So that even more hairs can be grown,
On Uncle Sam, the US of A.

And all of that oil and maybe even more,
Has made the grease, right down to his core
And all of us toil,
So the US can get its oil,
But that's the way it's always worked,
For Uncle Sam, the US of A.

So from all that you have
Heard
You can easily
Tell
That the biggest bully in the
Playground is . . .
*Russia?*
So they say.

**Danny Munroe (12)**
**Dunbar Grammar School, Dunbar**

# Why?

Why would anyone do this?
What have I done wrong?
Did I make a mistake?
What should I not have done?

Must I change my life
Just to please their stupid game?
I don't want to play!
But still the game goes on

What's so funny about it?
It's nowhere near a joke
My misery has turned into a comedy
How could they stoop so low?

My friends have deserted me
Because of fear and cowardice
They're scared they'll be taunted too
Why did I call them friends?

What's the point of it?
But I guess it doesn't matter now
You see, I'm in Heaven
Far away from them now.

**Julie Huggan (13)**
**Dunbar Grammar School, Dunbar**

## The Polluted World

The world is a big and beautiful place,
But humans are turning it into a disgrace
And with these words I want you to understand,
That we can still save this wonderful land.

Pollution is deadly, it can easily spread,
Spread like butter onto bread.
It kills animals and pollutes the air,
You wouldn't throw away your litter if you really did care.

September the 11th two thousand and one
When all the pain and damage was done.
It happened so easily, it was all so quick,
Like a toddler knocking over a tower of bricks.

If you want to help the world, then do as I say,
It's not too late if you start today.
Think of terrorism and the problem with pollution
And together we will find the perfect solution.

**Katharine Duguid (12)**
**Dunbar Grammar School, Dunbar**

## I Have A Dream

I have a dream
Where there's sunshine
And blue skies
All the time

I have a dream
Where no one's starving
Everyone has food
And everyone's charming

I have a dream
Where no one's alone
Everyone's loved
And always talking on the phone

I have a dream
Where everyone's delighted
To be in this world
And always excited

I have a dream
Where there's no bad drugs
Criticism, racism
Or back street thugs

So now I hope you understand
What's in this world
And across the land

Together we can make my dream come true
With help from me
And help from you.

**Debbie Moore (13)**
**Gourock High School, Gourock**

## I Have A Dream

I have a dream,
Where people don't get bullied,
Where people don't get made fun of,
Where they all get along.

I have a dream,
Where people don't blame themselves,
Where they don't hurt themselves,
Where they feel accepted.

I have a dream,
Where everyone is happy,
Where no one is left out,
Where there is no hatred.

I live in a world,
Where people get bullied,
Where people get made fun of,
Where people don't get along.

I live in a world,
Where people blame themselves,
Where people hurt themselves,
Where they don't feel accepted.

I live in a world,
Where not everyone is happy,
Where someone is left out,
Where there is hatred

I preferred my dream.

**Peter Nimmo (14)**
**Gourock High School, Gourock**

## Open The Window

A window in the world,
To see deeper.
Imagine it.
To see the wrongs and the rights,
The life and the death.
Think about it.
Flashed-by-never-to-return childhoods,
Cut short by violence.
Imagine it.
Smoke rising from the chimneys of cities,
Choking the world.
Think about it.
See the problems,
See the solutions.
Imagine it.
The answers are there,
We can use them.
Think about it.
Let us open the window
Now we have seen deeper.
Imagine it.
Peace and silence surging back
As the gunfire is ceased.
Think about it.
And the hush is broken,
By joyous singing -
The world beautiful again.
Don't imagine it.
Don't think about it.
Let's just make it happen.

**Andrew Clark (13)**
**Gourock High School, Gourock**

## I Have A Dream

I have a dream that animal cruelty will stop.

I have a dream that one day,
Or today, child abuse will stop
And that children will grow up
And not be forced to take drugs
And have to be attacked for possessions.

I have a dream that racism will be banned
And that we can be friends
And get along with each other.

I have a dream that crime will stop
And the punishment will be more cruel
To the killers and attackers and so on.

I have a dream that one day
We will all get treated equally
And that we can all afford food.

**Robyn Govier**
**Porthcawl Comprehensive School, Porthcawl**

## I Have A Dream!

I have a dream, a dream about us.
I have a dream, a dream about a child.
I dream this dream every day and night.
How this child gets beaten,
How this child gets hurt.
I wonder how we can stop this,
I wonder, will it carry on?
But I will put a stop to it,
A stop to the terrible crime.
Just think how many children there are
Getting scared and suicidal,
Are you going to let it carry on?
Please make it stop.

**Corey Bridgeman (13)**
**Porthcawl Comprehensive School, Porthcawl**

## I Have A Dream

I have a dream that animals won't be abused,
I have a dream that there won't be any more suffering for animals.
I have a dream that people won't kill animals to make money.
I have a dream that animals will not be sent to the zoo.
I have a dream that animals can stay in their habitat
And be peaceful where they come from.

I have a dream that animals will be left alone
To make a family and do natural things.

I have a dream.

**Luke Nicholas (12)**
**Porthcawl Comprehensive School, Porthcawl**

## Peace

I have a dream that terrorism will be gone
And there will be peace.
I have a dream that war will come to an end
And the soldiers can go and have a life.

I have a dream that violence and crimes
Shall be ended so people won't be scared
To walk outside their houses
Without being shot or attacked.

I have a dream that
There will be peace,
We want an end to violence.
We want an end.

**Nick Gillingham (12)**
**Porthcawl Comprehensive School, Porthcawl**

## I Have A Dream

I have a dream that child abuse will stop
And children will be happy,
That families will be together
So the world is a happier place.

I have a dream that everyone will be kind
And we all help stop child abuse happening
And just support children all the way.

I have a dream that anyone can help them.

**Courtney Sims (12)**
**Porthcawl Comprehensive School, Porthcawl**

## I Have A Dream

I have a dream that one day the nations should think
About the Third World countries
And they would get more attention.
We all should have the same rights to live life
And be happy not negative.

I have a dream that we should not take advantage
Of all the different foods and choice that we have.
I believe that there will be a lot of people
Who would sacrifice at least a loaf of bread.

I have a dream that states that are rich will really think
About the terrible things that happen in this world.
They might not realise what people go through being poor.

I have a dream that in the future we will be equal
And we will all have a chance in life.
To be happy and have a family like most people do.
Don't take advantage of what you've got!

I have a dream!

**Nicole Robbins (12)**
**Porthcawl Comprehensive School, Porthcawl**

## I Have A Dream

I have a dream that animal cruelty will be in the history books.
That people will care for other living things.
My dream is that fox hunts will be frowned upon by everyone.
I have a dream that man traps and guns will be locked in an iron safe.
My dream is for fish not to swim in polluted seas.
My dream is for snakes not to be killed.
I have a dream that orang-utans will live without fear.
I have a dream that a circus with animals will fade from memories.
My dream is for animals to be treated as we like to be
treated ourselves.
My dream is that beings that fly, swim and crawl will be free from terror
Forever.

That's my dream!

**Bethanie Denyer (12)**
**Porthcawl Comprehensive School, Porthcawl**

## I Dream!

I have a dream!

I dream of a world without bullying.

I dream!

That one day, all children should be free
And able to live without terror.

That one day, children won't have to go to hospital
With serious injuries caused by bullies.

I have a dream!

I dream that all children can hold hands together
And live in harmony.

I dream!

I dream, that parents will not bombard their children with assaults.

I dream parents will learn to accept their children.

I have a dream!

I dream of a world without bullying.

I have a dream!

**Owain Morgan (13)**
**Porthcawl Comprehensive School, Porthcawl**

## I Have A Dream

I have a dream that one day
There will be no bullying existing in this world,
That every child will have the right to be able
To go to school without feeling broken-hearted, lonely, neglected
And will have the right to be able to take part in everything.

I have a dream that children will feel safe
When they walk through the door of their home
And not get beaten by abusive parents.

I have a dream that all of God's children
Can rise together and feel equally important
About themselves and each other.
All children should be treated with respect.

I have a dream that we will find love in the bottom of our hearts
And make each other feel good about ourselves.

**Jade Wallis (13)**
**Porthcawl Comprehensive School, Porthcawl**

## I Had A Dream

One day I had a dream that we will all be free.
Free from poverty, free from sickness, free from racism.
I had a dream that we would all be free.

One day I had a dream that we will have the answers to life,
The universe and everything.
I had a dream that we knew.

One day I had a dream that people know not of hate,
That they love and cherish each other.
I had a dream that we know not of hate.

One day I had a dream that the world was perfect,
Free of everything bad, a paradise, a utopia, a perfect place.
I had a dream but that's all it was . . .
. . . a dream.

**Rhys Thomas (13)**
**Porthcawl Comprehensive School, Porthcawl**

## I Have A Dream - Words To Change The World

I have a dream that one day this world,
The whole world, will unite together as one.
That there will be no wars or famine, no hunger or greed.
That all people shall be treated as equal.
From western to eastern people, from northern to southern people.
After all, we are all people - humans.
God made us different colours, different shapes and sizes.
We have different beliefs and thoughts,
But that does not make us different.
We should all accept the beliefs of others
And have no war between us.
I have a dream that the world will change,
But the only way it will change is because of us.
Only we can change it!

I have a dream.

**James Harris (13)**
**Porthcawl Comprehensive School, Porthcawl**

## Unreachable?

I have a dream that one day terrorism and crime come to a halt.
When all people realise the consequences
of their intentions and decisions.
When the colour and religion of just a single person
makes no difference to the world's dictation.

I have a dream that one day all firearms and weapons
are exiled from every house and hand.
No war or terrorism will resurrect after being laid to rest.
Perseverance is a must if the people of the world want all time peace.

I have a dream that one day all acts of terrorism
will be brought to surface, that all involved
pay a price for justice for others and themselves.
That people indulge themselves in self-righteousness
and not wrong doing.

I have a dream that one day murderous acts
and gunnings become extinct and all people believe
that with time, help and faith, all will be forgotten and forgiven.

But is this dream too much?
Too late . . . and unreachable?

I don't think so.

**Jade Bickerstaff (13)**
**Porthcawl Comprehensive School, Porthcawl**

## I Have A Dream

As I sit down and think about life,
I think about war and crime and misery.
'How sad! How sad!' I say to myself,
How sad this is what the world has come to!

But I have a dream,
A dream for the world!
My dream is for all, for peace on the Earth!

I want for the world,
What I want for me!
Freedom and harmony and no more war.
For war is despicable,
A terrible thing,
No one deserves to fight for others,
Stand up for each other.
No one deserves to take the blame for others' mistakes;
Face the consequences.

My dream is for him and her and them.
My dream is for us and we and you.
This is my dream, do you want it too?

**Georgina Evans (11)**
**Porthcawl Comprehensive School, Porthcawl**

## My Dream

I have a dream, a powerful dream,
One that will change the world.
My dream is that life will be consistent.

Why do people have to end their lives for no reason at all?

My dream will not only benefit one person,
But everyone around them.
It will bring peace and rid the world of poverty and stress.
Disease and disabilities will be no more
When my dream comes true.

In future years this planet will be empty
Thanks to terrorism, guns and death.

If my dream comes true,
No one will die.
Murders and suicides will not exist,
When my dream comes true.

When my dream comes true,
Choirs will sing,
Fireworks will set the sky alight.
Everyone will be happy.

Close your eyes and think,
Think about life beyond death.
No one knows what it is,
We can only imagine it.

Imagine if my dream came true,
You wouldn't have to think about it.
Think, think, think.
Close your eyes and think,
Think about my dream
Of a consistent life.

That is my dream, my wish, my desire.

**Georgina Dorr (11)**
**Porthcawl Comprehensive School, Porthcawl**

## My Dream,

I have a dream,
To swim the oceans,
Raging blue,
To save the dolphins, whales too,
Play with them and give them hope,
Free them from the vicious nets
And bring them safely home.

I have a dream,
To walk the planes,
Dusty and dry,
To save elephants and giraffes 30 feet high,
Give them hope of finding their families,
Save them from the poacher's gun
And release them to the wild.

I have a dream,
To explore the jungle,
All lush and green,
To save gorillas hidden not to be seen,
Give them back their homes,
Rescue them from falling trees
And give them what they need.

I have a dream,
That people like you,
Will help me stop animal cruelty
And give animals what they deserve,
Please make my dream come true!

**Cheryl McAndrew (12)**
**Porthcawl Comprehensive School, Porthcawl**

## My Dream

I have a dream that all children will be treated the same.
Don't make fun of that boy because of his name.
Don't make fun of her because of her dress.
That boy's kind, so what if he plays chess?
Children shouldn't be judged by the way they look.
Science club, looking at a library book.

I have a dream that bullies don't control the playground,
Take children's pocket money, 'Come on, it's just a pound.'
'Sticks and stones may break my bones,
But names will never hurt me.'
It's not all true,
Names can hurt you.

I have a dream that children big or small,
Will not get beaten up by someone tall.

I have a dream of children standing free,
Alongside me!

**Alex Nia Howells (11)**
**Porthcawl Comprehensive School, Porthcawl**

## I Have A Dream

I have a dream
That could help save the Earth.

Just do a little something;
Lead others by example.
Recycle as you go
To help save the Earth.

Glass bottles that have been used,
And never will be again,
Could be put forward for another purpose
To help save the Earth.

Newspapers that have just been read
And are full of yesterday's news
Could be used for another purpose
That could help save the Earth.

And even as we do this,
We are helping our forests too.
Don't cut down all our trees
And help save the Earth.

It wouldn't take much effort
If we all tried our best.
Just do a little something
That could help save the Earth.

**Sophie Howe (11)**
**Porthcawl Comprehensive School, Porthcawl**

## I Have A Dream

I had a dream of a child crying out,
His eyes were filled with fear and doubt.
I had a dream of hunger and pain,
Crimes were committed again and again.

I had a dream that nobody cared,
For the man in the corner, lonely and scared.
I had a dream of a polluted world,
Poisonous gases and dangers unfurled.

I had a dream of poverty and war,
I have a dream that this be no more.
I have a dream of a world full of hope,
When in times of trouble, we'd be able to cope.

I have a dream that no more people will die,
No longer a reason for children to cry.
I have a dream that people are free,
We'll all live together in harmony.

I have a dream where we all live in unison,
This world, not ours, would be my decision.

**Rachel Tayler (12)**
**Porthcawl Comprehensive School, Porthcawl**

## Inequality Of Souls

Walk down the corridor of humiliation and rejection
Sit in the classroom of laughter and hurt
Roam the playground of constant apprehension
And live the life of souls they've burnt.

Think why they judge you on your personal beliefs
Question why they force you to cry yourself to sleep
Ask how faultless they can be
And how badly they assume what you really mean.

Wonder why the force, the feeling of antonyms towards you
Conceive the fact that how inanimate they're willing to be
Conclude the birch the feeling in your heart
Why, why do they do this?

**Emma Bold (13)**
**Porthcawl Comprehensive School, Porthcawl**

## If Only They Had A Dream

I have a dream that one day, one day the people of the world
will rise up and say *no* to war.
I have a dream that there will be a day
when mothers, brothers, sisters, cousins
won't have to grieve over their loved ones.
I have a dream that people won't fight,
but rejoice the different religions of the world,
every person's colour, view, dream.
I have a dream that war will stop
and the children of the war will be able
to play freely in the streets.
I have a dream, that world leaders will
think, think, just think of what it must be like
to return to your home, a mass grave.
And stop this craziness of war.
I have a dream that one day, one day
the people of the world will rise up and say
*No* to war.
But it's one person's dream, my dream
and that can't change the world, so
I have a dream that the whole world
would dream that war would stop.
Then we could stop it, then we would stop it.
Stop it now, together, united.
If only, if only they had a dream.

**Charlotte Wardman (13)**
**Porthcawl Comprehensive School, Porthcawl**

## My Wish And Dream

I have a dream, one day terror will finish,
the endless waiting and anticipation of death will be over.
I have a dream that terror will not get in the way
of our lives and our children's lives.
I have a dream that one day
we will walk proudly down unknown streets
and not worry what's around the corner.
I have a dream that one day
there will be no more broadcasting of evil
and no destructive gossip.
I have a dream that one day
the world will become truly united.
I have a dream that one day
people will stand up for what is right
and will not be quiet when evil spreads
its dark wing over us.
And we will all join together to
remove this terror from this wonderful planet.

**Rebecca Thomas (13)**
**Porthcawl Comprehensive School, Porthcawl**

## I Have A Dream

I have a dream that one day all of Earth's countries
will be united as one.
That there will be no wars and battles,
no greed or hunger.

I have a dream that one day
Earth will be able to act as one big family.
Work together as a team and help one another.

I have a dream that one day
terrorism will come to an end.
No planning to invade each other,
no bombs and guns, but only peace and harmony.

I have a dream that one day
people will trust each other from all corners of the globe.
I dream of friendship and trust.

I have a dream that I hope others will follow!

I have a dream that one day
all religions will bind together,
we shall all believe in all religions.

Thank you, immortal God! We are free at last!

**Thomas Leach (13)**
**Porthcawl Comprehensive School, Porthcawl**

## Global Warming

The Earth is warming up
The ice is melting down
So if you don't recycle
The polar bears will drown

The ice is the home
For a polar bear
So turn off the lights
To show you care

Don't use aerosols
Or even spray
Because if you do
The world will pay.

**Roisin Evans (11)**
**Porthcawl Comprehensive School, Porthcawl**

## I Have A Dream

I have a dream, that one day, people will realise what we are doing to this beautiful planet.

This is my future, your future, our children's future,
our children's children's future.
Why are we throwing it away? We only get one world
and it's up to us to take care of it and to teach the future generations
the importance of taking care of this wonderful planet we live on.

If we could only see all of the pollution which is suffocating the world.
Which is penetrating the air around us
and damaging the rich soil beneath our feet.
The shield of ozone armour, which protects us
from the rays of the sun, is being slowly chiselled away at,
by the pollution that we are creating.

I fear that by the time that our children's children's children
arrive in this Earth, there will be nothing left for them.
The Earth will be barren and bare. No life or plants to grow.
Hardly any fresh water to drink. I picture it, as grey and dirty.
No plants. No animals. No life. Nothing.

My dream is that people will realise the damage we are causing.
Everybody can help to save the world, everybody can dream
my dream and everybody can save energy and recycle more.

I have a dream, that one day,
the world will be a beautiful and peaceful one,
which we have helped to preserve, protect and care for.

Only you and I can make my dream . . . a reality.

**Kathryn Allen (12)**
**Porthcawl Comprehensive School, Porthcawl**

## I Have A Dream

I have a dream that one day bullying will stop,
Children should not be scared of going into school.
All children have rights to be happy.
They should not fear another person.
Parents should not scare their child.
Children have a right to go into school happy.
They should be able to go out without being scared.
Children should not be scared.

I have a dream that bullying should stop.
All bullies are often sad.
Let bullies not bully.
Let them be happy at home.
Bullies are often found hurting another.
They are also found hurting themselves.

I have a dream that all bullies and victims,
Become friends.
Give them all help.
Children should be able to love each other,
Not hate another.
Let parents support their child,
Not make them sad.

**Hannah Gibbins (13)**
**Porthcawl Comprehensive School, Porthcawl**

## I Have A Dream

I have a dream there won't be charities for child abuse in Africa,
Not because we can't afford them, but because we don't need them.
There's enough food and water to spread around this world,
So why isn't it?
I have a dream that one day there is enough peace
and happiness to spread around every person on this planet,
enemies turning into friends, families and siblings turning
into 'best mates' as well as being a part of your life.
I have a dream that one day, war will be almost a swear word,
where it is foul to say it or even mention it,
not because there is an unwanted amount of strife,
but because there isn't such a thing as it anymore,
it's all in the past.
I have a dream that one day children won't be worried
or afraid of something or someone.
They won't hesitate to go to school,
they will go from their own free will and pleasure.
I have a dream that one day there will be more
joy and peace in this world than sadness and tears
and nothing could stop our hopes and dreams.

**Katrina Davies (12)**
**Porthcawl Comprehensive School, Porthcawl**

## I Have A Dream

I have a dream that one day the world will give children a chance.
That elder people give children a chance.
To make sure no child is afraid of their own home,
To make sure no child is afraid of their own school.
We must stop child abuse!

I have a dream that one day those children
Should live the life they deserve,
That children can enjoy a life like the ones who aren't abused.
To make sure children are treated almost equally,
To make sure children are treated with the respect they deserve.
We too can make a difference in the world!

**Rebecca Jones (13)**
**Porthcawl Comprehensive School, Porthcawl**

## I Have A Dream . . .

I have a dream that one day
money will not be the solution to everything
and everyone's problems in life.
That people's greed will not be
the downfall of humanity all together.
That everyone will get a fair share
of what they deserve.
I have a dream that one day
war will end and people will work together
to create a better world
without greed, poverty and war.
I have a dream that people will learn
from their mistakes and be sorry for
what they have done to other people's lives
and what effect it had had on the world.

I have a dream that one day
my dream will come true.

**Elliott Jenkins (12)**
**Porthcawl Comprehensive School, Porthcawl**

## I Have A Dream!

I have a dream that bullying will be a thing of the past.
That I will be able to walk to school with all my friends,
Without getting picked on by older school pupils.

I have a dream that I will be able to sit in a class,
With no one calling one names and stealing my stuff
And that people won't throw things at me.

I have a dream that I will be able to be in the playground,
With lots of friends and no one tripping me up
And no one will be horrible to me.

I have a dream that there will be no bullying!

**Ashleigh Furness (13)**
**Porthcawl Comprehensive School, Porthcawl**

## I Have A Dream

I have a dream that I could wake up in the morning
without worrying about any bullying.
I have a dream that there was no violence
or harm in other human beings.
I have a dream that everyone
could just get on with each other.

I have a dream that black people
and white people could live together,
be together without being made fun of.

I have a dream that crime vanished
no longer to be heard of.

**Josh Prescott (13)**
**Porthcawl Comprehensive School, Porthcawl**

## I Have A Dream

I have a dream, that when I walk outside one day
I will breathe in fresh air and there will be no pollution in the air.

I have a dream, that when I walk through the street
I won't have to see rubbish between my toes.
I won't have to look up into the sky
To see black clouds of steam instead of clear blue skies.

I have a dream, that people will start to
Take care of everything around them
And we could take control of global warming and stop it.

I have a dream.

**Matthew Evans (13)**
**Porthcawl Comprehensive School, Porthcawl**

## I Have A Dream

That when I wake up there will be no child abuse,
That the world will be free of all bullying.
Parents will wake up and protect their children,
There will no longer be children in danger.

There are some parents that leave their children to starve,
There are some parents that hit them
Until they are battered and bruised.
There are other parents that throw them out on the street alone,
What is the point in having kids if you will abuse them?

I have a dream
That parents look after their children and give them good lives,
Some parents don't even give the effort
To clean them or dress them.

Can we stop child abuse?

**Angharad Davies (12)**
**Porthcawl Comprehensive School, Porthcawl**

## I Had A Dream

I had a dream that one day
I wouldn't have to go to school
And be pressurised to give my lunch away.

I had a dream that one day
I wouldn't come home with tears running down my face
From bullies punching me.

I had a dream that one time
I would wake up with no one telling me
That it's going to be alright when they know it's not
They're just trying to make me feel better
Until that day comes.

I had a dream that no one would
Call me names like four eyes
Just because I wear glasses
Or pick on me just because of the way I look.

I had a dream that one day
People would become friends with me
Instead of staring at me, whispering about the way I am
I can only be me, why can't anybody understand that?

I'm just me!

**Nia Challenger (12)**
**Porthcawl Comprehensive School, Porthcawl**

## My Poem

I have a dream
That when I wake up and open my curtains
I can see people walking around
And bike riding to work
Speaking happily to each other on their way
I wish the world was at peace
And so were we with each other.

I have a dream
That no matter what colour skin we have
Or what clothes we wear
We could give each other the freedom
And opportunity there is
I wish that we would stop killing our world
With pollution, vandalism and wars
What is the point?
In life we are all one, brothers and sisters
Friends and family
Why cause pain, heartache and sadness?

I have a dream
But will that dream ever come true?

I have a dream
That animals can walk free and live happy
And we would not kill them for fun
Or keep them in captivity for our own fun
Don't be cruel, be kind.

I have a dream
But will that dream ever come true?

**Abigail Weale (13)**
**Porthcawl Comprehensive School, Porthcawl**

# I Have A Dream That There Will Be No Poverty In The World

One day I hope that in Africa and in the Middle East
The people will have fresh water to drink.

One day I hope that in these poor places
They have the healthy food we have here in Britain.

One day I hope that in these poor places
All the people have clean clothes and shoes on their feet.

One day I hope that the people in poor countries
Have the luxuries that we have in Britain

And then maybe one day the world will be perfect.

**Sam Williams (13)**
**Porthcawl Comprehensive School, Porthcawl**

## I Have A Dream . . .

For animals to have loving homes,
Not left outside with broken bones.

People buy them from a home,
But realise they don't want them
And leave them all alone.

Then they hit them and say,
'I wish I never had that thing.'
I know I should dump it in a bin.

Then they never feed it
And it gets skinnier and skinnier
And abuse it until it can hardly move.

But then one day, they dump them in an alley,
Hoping someone will come and get them
And take them home.

Then they are skinny and very depressed
And try to find food, all wet and cold.

If they are then lucky - and most are,
A kind person or NCDL will take them in their car.

Be fed, until they're a perfect size
And get attention and be happy
For as long as they live.

**Emma Hill (13)**
**Porthcawl Comprehensive School, Porthcawl**

## I Have A Dream

I have a dream that child abuse is stopped,
I have a dream that the abusers are locked up,
I have a dream that the children are put in caring homes,
I have a dream that they are loved and never unhappy again.

I have a dream,
I have a dream.

**Amy Rhys (12)**
**Porthcawl Comprehensive School, Porthcawl**

## I Had A Dream

I had a dream
There was no bullying in the world
And people weren't afraid to walk
Out of the door they felt no suffering
And no sadness
Instead they held their head high
And got on with their life
Without having to look over their shoulders
And see people behind, making fun and throwing stones
There would be none of this anymore
No woman, man or child should go through this pain
There would be none of this anymore
None of this!

**Jacob Chappell (13)**
**Porthcawl Comprehensive School, Porthcawl**

## I Have A Dream That There Will Be No Pollution In The World!

I have a dream
That there will be no pollution in the world
That people can walk out of the front door
And breathe in fresh, clean air

I have a dream
That people will start walking to work
Instead of using cars
Which give off fumes and pollute the air

I have a dream
That people will stop throwing rubbish
In our clean rivers

I have a dream
That people will stop polluting
Our beautiful world.

**Kelly Ann Dyde (13)**
**Porthcawl Comprehensive School, Porthcawl**

## I Have A Dream . . .

I have a dream that this world is free of war,
If there were not any wars this world would be
Wonderful and full of peace,
I dream that all fighting and bombing will cease.

I have a dream that this world is free of war,
I wish the guns and bombs were no more.
I dream that people will treat others
The exact way they want to be treated,
If people treated others as well as they should,
Then this world would be free!
Let freedom enter to every country!
Let freedom ring to all people!
Let freedom ring all the world!

Freedom! Freedom!
Let it ring!
Let it enter!
Free at last! Free at last!

**Josie Loye (12)**
**Porthcawl Comprehensive School, Porthcawl**

## I Have A Dream

I have a dream that one day there will be
No war or hatred and all people can go outside
Without the fear of getting hurt
No countries will be locked in war with each other.

I have a dream that one day
People won't be dying for their country in war
And there won't be innocent people dying in cities
Being bombed by planes and rockets.

I have a dream that one day there won't be
Gangs of people ganging up on other people
And there won't be any need for ASBOs or jail
There won't be any racism and we won't need the police.

I have a dream that we could be free from war if we tried.

**Jak Kent (13)**
**Porthcawl Comprehensive School, Porthcawl**

## I Have A Dream

I have a dream that poverty will be made history
And all the people in the world will be happy
And live a great life.
Poverty will stop if we all pull together
And help each other.
When you throw the rest of your rice in the bin, think,
It can feed one person in Africa for one week.

I have a dream that in one year
The word 'poverty' will be said no more.
If most footballers cut their pay in half and gave it to Africa,
Then the people in Africa could live longer.
Everybody in the world deserves to make the best of life.
We can stop poverty if we try hard.
The *we* is us; the world.

I have a dream to make poverty history.

**Lewis Jones (12)**
**Porthcawl Comprehensive School, Porthcawl**

## I Have A Dream

I have a dream to stop cruelty to animals
That animals will be looked after
And their owners will earn to look after their pets
And stop people from hunting animals

I have a dream that all animal cruelty will end
And suffering will become a thing of the past

I have a dream that people's animals
Will live and get well and not be killed
But live as they grow old

I have a dream that people's animals
Will be treated well, not hit and unfed
But make them healthy

I have a dream that puppies and kittens
Should not be left alone and not be abandoned
But be looked after properly

I wish that animals will be looked after
And be well for always.

**Samantha Hopkins (12)**
**Porthcawl Comprehensive School, Porthcawl**

## Untitled

I have a dream that the world
will no longer be scared
by weapons and wars

I have a dream that we will no longer
fear terrorism and violence

I have a dream that justice will prevail
in the world

I have a dream that murder will become
a thing of the past

I have a dream that peace can be brought
to the world.

**Andrew McQueen (12)**
**Porthcawl Comprehensive School, Porthcawl**

## I Have A Dream

I have a dream that everyone
will be treated the same.
I have a dream that
we can live in peace.

I have a dream that
there will be no more
hatred in the world.

I have a dream that
people will not be
prejudiced to people
because of their race.

I have a dream that
people will learn to love
each other.

**Imogen Lewis-Davidson (13)**
**Porthcawl Comprehensive School, Porthcawl**

## I Have A Dream

I have a dream that one day
The animals being abused will be free
From all nasty people in the world

I have a dream that all animals
Will have a warm, loving home
Not living on the streets
Or in houses where they will be abused

I have a dream that all animals will be happy
They will have enough food
Not have to look through bins
Or go without food

I have a dream

I have a dream that all animals
Used for animal testing
Will be set free and not used

I have a dream that all animals
In cages will be let into the wild

I have a dream that all animals
Like monkeys, kept as pets and kept
In awful conditions will be free

Free to have fun with their own kind
Not kept in small cages
And in their own waste

I have a dream that this will happen
Hopefully it *will* happen.

**Lizzie Crocker (13)**
**Porthcawl Comprehensive School, Porthcawl**

## I Have A Dream!

I have a dream that no one will be rich
And no one will be poor
The world will all have the same

I have a dream that everyone will have a home
No longer be on the streets
And no one will have a mansion

I have a dream that everyone will have
The same amount of money
And the same amount of land.

I have a dream that no one will be poor
And no one will be rich
We all have to share the same things.

**Chelsea Gatter (12)**
**Porthcawl Comprehensive School, Porthcawl**

## I Have A Dream!

I have a dream that people
Will stand up for children
So there is no child abuse in the world

I have a dream that children
Will not suffer in silence and be hurt for nothing
People should support the NSPCC to help the children

I have a dream that one day in our lifetime
Children will not have to run away
They should ring the NSPCC for advice

Stand up! Stand up!

**Leah Richards (11)**
**Porthcawl Comprehensive School, Porthcawl**

## I Have A Dream

I have a dream to stop cruelty to children.
I have a dream that one day
children will be able to play safely out in the streets.
I have a dream that one day
parents will start treating children
like they are a part of their lives.
I have a dream that one day
adults can play with their children
and children can think they're safe with their parents.
I have a dream that one day
children can grow up without any cruelty to them.
I have a dream that one day
children can feel safe and go out
without anyone bullying them.

**Drew Richards (12)**
**Porthcawl Comprehensive School, Porthcawl**

## I Have A Dream

I have a dream that one day cruelty will stop
and suffering will become a thing of the past.
I have a dream the animals can be treated
how we would like to be.
Animals are being treated badly
and most people don't care.
Animals are not treated with respect
and the worse they are treated
the more likely they are to run away.
I have a dream that animals will be cared for and fed
and if so the world will be a much better place.
I have a dream animals will be happy
even though we cannot talk to them.

**Lauren Jones (12)**
**Porthcawl Comprehensive School, Porthcawl**

## I Have A Dream

I have a dream that all wars will be stopped,
that the mass weapons will be locked away
and peace will rule our world.

I have a dream that soldiers will go home
and be used again and people will not have to live in fear.

I have a dream that no bio weapons will ever be used again
and people will not have to live in fear.

I have a dream that terrorism will no longer exist
and people will not have to throw their lives away.

I have a dream that beautiful land will not be destroyed
by our weapons and flowers will be placed instead.

I have a dream that all wars will be stopped.

**Connor Moody (11)**
**Porthcawl Comprehensive School, Porthcawl**

## I Have A Dream

I have a dream that people will be treated the same
and not made to feel unwanted or unwelcome because of their colour.

I have a dream that people will be treated equally
because that's all they want, not treated better, just the same.

I have a dream that people won't be bullied or abused
mentally or physically because of their colour.

I have a dream that in the future people will realise
that we are all the same on the inside
and that there isn't any difference between us on the inside
and that is what maters, not what colour skin we have.

It doesn't matter if we are black or white,
there is enough room in the world for us!
But not enough for racism!

**Charlotte Tasker (11)**
**Porthcawl Comprehensive School, Porthcawl**

## I Have A Dream

I have a dream that one day people will treat others the same.
Just because we are different religion and different colour,
It does not mean we have to treat others differently.

We all have hearts, we all have the same blood
Flowing through our veins.
If we are all the same on the inside
Why do we treat others differently?
I wish one day we will all join hands and pray.

Children get bullied because of their skin colour.
So what if they are different, they can all play football or tag.
Just because they look different doesn't mean
They can't all do the same as you.

Please, for our world, let there be peace!

**Rebecca Maddern (11)**
**Porthcawl Comprehensive School, Porthcawl**

## I Have A Dream

I have a dream
That one day, some time in the future,
There will be no wars, no lack of respect for our neighbours,
That no longer will the war-scarred countries
Hear the unforgettable scream of a child running from its 'captors.'
That no longer will a person be left alone to grieve over
Their irreplaceable family.

I have a dream
That never again will the great minds of the world
Scheme and plot for new ways to hurt and kill
The innocent lives around them.
That no man may ever have the power to take the dreams of a child
And shatter their lives before them.

I have a dream
That the manufacturing of arms and weapons
Which fuel the destruction of war will forever cease to exist.
That the cold-blooded surge inside us that drives us to do wrong
May be swallowed back and tossed to where it may never return.

I have a dream
Which is mine to hold, that all the anger and hatred in the world
Should be banished, that we can trust one another
And respect them like our brother or sister.
That we can now realise we all bleed the same blood
And we all breathe the same air and the world is here for us to share
And we can live in peace together!

**Nathan Gillingham (13)**
**Porthcawl Comprehensive School, Porthcawl**

## I Have A Dream

I have a dream
A dream where people in Africa and other Third World countries
Have the same freedom and rights as people from countries
as rich and wealthy as ours.
Where people can go to school to get educated.
Where children are able to use the simple but effective equipment
enabling them to learn and get a good education.
Where people can earn more than just enough
to support their families and their needs.
Where rich and poor have not got such a gap of status.
Where poverty is a thing of the past and development is the future.
I have a dream where people in Third World countries all live in houses.
Houses to give them comfort and warmth.
They shouldn't be sleeping on the streets.
They shouldn't be sleeping in boxes
or mud huts which will fall down from a half strong wind.
No, because I had a dream where all people had equal rights.
Where people got at least the standard minimum wage.
Where children from Third World countries
got the same privileges as our children get.
Where there was only first world countries.
I have a dream and that dream is to get rid of poverty, full stop.
Poverty is the world's number one problem and killer.
Someone dies every three seconds.
We can change the world, so why don't we?

**Shelley Heanue (12)**
**Porthcawl Comprehensive School, Porthcawl**

## I Have A Dream - My Dream

I have a dream that no child will be born
into a world of religious prejudice.
They will not know the scorn and hate between two religions.
They will stand side by side.

I have a dream that all people can worship together,
in the same country, all over the world.
They will accept each other's faiths and understand each other.

The pain and hate of terrorism will end.
Women and men would be free to preach on the streets - side by side.

Everyone will realise that there is only one religion -
just in a thousand different versions.
We all share this world together.

The Christians, the Jews and the Buddhists.
The Protestants, the Hindus and the pagans and even the atheists
will realise we share this world - and we will stand together -
side by side.

I have a dream . . .
My dream.

**Tahlia Platts (13)**
**Porthcawl Comprehensive School, Porthcawl**

## I Have A Dream

I have a dream that this world will discover the meaning of peace
which will flood our nation wide.
I have a dream that one day terrorism will cease to exist
throughout our land and the fast of vicious bombings will be forgotten.
I have a dream that one day we will become a nation
where racist remarks towards people will not be tolerated.
I have a dream of a beautiful country, where the women and children
are not in poverty and are treated equally, not judged by
what they may look like but by their inner soul and true character.
I have a dream where little children are able to go
to their own school and not have to fight for justice
of being bullied because they are different.
I have a dream where war cannot be declared in any island
or country but instead peace is declared throughout
the whole of the Earth.

**Roberto Rossini (12)**
**Porthcawl Comprehensive School, Porthcawl**

## I Have A Dream

I have a dream that all countries
from America to Japan to Australia will join hands,
no matter what the colour of their skin or what god they believe in
and help the Third World countries stop being Third World countries
and start being countries that are happy and free.
I have a dream that children everywhere have the right
to a free education and that they are not ridiculed or hated
because they don't look the same or they sound different.
Where is the love in this world? Because I can't see it.
I can't see happiness, I can't see united countries
and I can't see countries being kind.
All I see and hear on the television and in the newspaper
is murder, racism, poverty and war.
This should stop. This should stop now before it's too late.
This world will destroy itself, tear itself to pieces little by little,
country by country and all God's wonderful work will be wasted.
We were not created to hate and kill,
we were created to love and be loved by others
but we don't, not all of us care about the world,
not all of us care about other people.
I have a dream that this all changed.
Maybe not today, maybe not tomorrow but someday soon.
I dream we will all come together and help each other
live and be happy.
I have a dream that the world will be united.
I have a dream I hope will come true.

**Alice Power (13)**
**Porthcawl Comprehensive School, Porthcawl**

## I Dream Of Harmony

I have a dream that one day God's Earth
will be overrun with plants and animals
and not with skyscrapers that touch the sky
but trees instead.

I have a dream that one day Man will be able to live
alongside all God's creatures,
that Man will not kill for fur and tusks
but will be able to turn away from greed.

I have a dream that one day we will consider
that plants grow and animals feed
so that must mean they feel too,
they feel what we do to them.
The rainforest weeps as we cut her down,
we have to dry her tears.

I have a dream that one day
children will be born into an Earth
filled with thick, dense greenness
and the gentle babble of free animals
in their natural surroundings.
*This is my dream.*

**Hannah Brown (12)**
**Porthcawl Comprehensive School, Porthcawl**

## I Have A Dream

I have a dream, that one day all children will be able
To have a say in everything that goes on in their lives.
No matter what their age, they should not be scared
Of expressing their ideas.

I have a dream, that no matter what class children are from,
Whether it be upper class, middle or lower, all children
Should have equal rights in the form of education
And, no matter what their race or ability, will be happy.

I have a dream, that one day people will stop exploiting
Vulnerable children from the Far East,
Whose lives have been destroyed by disasters,
Yet Man creates a way to cause more mental destruction.
One day these children may be great leaders of this world,
But they will choose to do what they have experienced as acceptable.

I have a dream, that children will have a free, undisturbed
Mind and soul, that will develop with the necessary
And responsible guidance from their parents.
I believe that children will be exalted to the level of adults
And have equal rights!

I have a dream today!

**Ferdinand Ball (12)**
**Porthcawl Comprehensive School, Porthcawl**

## I Have A Dream

I have a dream that one day
no human will fear another.

I have a dream that one day
fighting will cease to exist
on this Earth.

I have a dream that one day
everyone on this Earth will have
the same rights and be able to say
what they think without being criticised.

I have a dream that one day
racism will stop and that
both black and white people
will live side by side.

I have a dream that one day
we will all live in peace and that
all evil things will be banished from this Earth
and only good things let to remain.

**Jonathan Phillips (13)**
**Porthcawl Comprehensive School, Porthcawl**

## I Have A Dream . . .

I have a dream that one day poverty will end.
That no person will have nothing.
That no child will cry with hunger or thirst.
That everyone will share what they have
And greed will not take over.
That no person will die for lack of food or clean water.

I have a dream we will all try.
Try to help others from suffering.
Suffering in poverty because of other people's greed.
There is enough food for everyone.
We will share.

I have a dream that one day
Every child will grow to be strong.
Strong enough to help others who may be in poverty.

I have a dream, a dream that might come true,
If only others can dream it too.
That's my dream and I will never give up.
Perseverance is everything.

**Rebecca Bates (12)**
**Porthcawl Comprehensive School, Porthcawl**

## War Will Cease

I have a dream that one day
the entire world will stand together in peace and harmony
and war will cease.
I have a dream that the people of the world,
black or white, Jew or Christian,
young or old, will stand together and say *no* to war,
world war, civil war, any war and war will cease.
I have a dream that the people of Iraq
will one day live in peace, with love and without hatred
and war will cease.
I have a dream that people will not kill for the fun of it.
No woman or man will die for being in the wrong place
at the wrong time!
*I have a dream that war will cease!*

**Rachel Ellis (12)**
**Porthcawl Comprehensive School, Porthcawl**

## Find The Light

From the cradle we find ourselves
Trapped.
Sheltered in the ignorant
Box of limited ideas,
We take our refuge.
Awake, we are tied, beaten to the ground
Like a dog, enslaved, child, chain,
But as we grow along the set path,
The knots thicken, weave and bind
So tightly that we are almost choked.
They crush our stars to dust
Till we become yet another clone.
Masked, we forget our individually
And lose it for what must seem an eternity.
We must fly free from the cliff,
The prison we built ourselves,
Leaving our sin behind us.

'Be like little children;'
For each child is a seed of hope.
We must not contain them
But water them in praise and encouragement
So that they grow,
Proud of their own shining colours,
Cherishing their uniqueness.

How else can we hope for a better future
If we chain the new generation to old prejudices?
Open your eyes,
Open your mind,
Open your heart and arms
To all the children of the world.

**Alice Jenkins (13)**
**Rye St Anthony School, Headington**

## I Have A Dream

I have many a dream.
I dream about making a difference.
I dream about making everyone friends.
Pictures slip through my mind;
I see a world free from insecurity;
A place where you feel safe.
As I walk down the street people stare, shamelessly.
They judge before they know.
I dream that I could make this not so.
And I dream I believe I can
And I dream I know I can.

As rain slips quietly down the window,
The tear-like drops tell a story.
I see children crying, dying, struggling to survive,
And I dream I could change this.
I dream I could save children from this.
Then I tell myself that I could, if I believe I can
And I dream I believe I can,
And I dream I know I can.

As I sit beneath the weeping willow,
I can hear it wailing,
I can feel its pain,
And as I write on this paper, I can see the tree,
The tree that was cut down and then processed.
I dream that I could save the tree,
Take it away from its misery,
Then I tell myself that I could, if I believe I can,
And I dream I believe I can,
And I dream I know I can.

**Eleanor Judges (12)**
**Rye St Anthony School, Headington**

# I Have A Dream

I have a dream,
I see a spaceship fly by his
Window and now I am gracefully floating
Above clouds of swirling mist. I look to him, the glow from the
Candles surrounding him, illuminating his face with a glow so strong,
He takes me to other lands and says to me,
'What I am is not real and what I am to you is not
What you mean to me.'
I follow him, on a journey through a strange but beautiful world,
It's nothing new; it's the only place I know.
Secretly, time stops moving and I can't sense one moment of it.
All I have is a dream, but in the dream I have him,
His hand guides me through curvaceous shapes in the shadows
And though I am dreaming, it seems real. I remember it so vividly,
And there are no explosions in this world.
I
Wake
From
The
Dream,
I see a bomb fly by his window, and there are explosions
In the real world.

**Natasha Turner (15)**
**Rye St Anthony School, Headington**

## Through A Dove's Eyes

I hear the cries of the young
I feel the pain of the people
I see the faces of suffering
I taste the bitter way of life.

So I try to call for help
But my words turn into whistles.
And these words cannot be heard
Not a word, not a word.

Oh why can't they understand?
I just want to give a hand
Oh voice where have you gone?
Need you to come along, to come along.

I sense the world is unbalanced
Words used for promises not kept
We must move on from the grief
Turn over a new leaf.

So I try to call for help
But my words turn into whistles.
And these words cannot be heard
Not a word, not a word.

Oh why can't they understand?
I just want to give a hand
Oh voice where have you gone?
Need you to come along, to come along.

**Natalie Balchin (17)**
**Rye St Anthony School, Headington**

## I Had A Dream

I had a dream
Where everything was peaceful,
I had a dream
Where everyone was kind,
I had a dream
Where no one was deaf,
I had a dream
Where no one was blind.

I had a dream
Where no one was racist,
I had a dream
Where no one was fascist,
I had a dream
Where no one was sexist,
I had a dream
Where no one was biased.

I had a dream
Where no one was judged by their looks,
I had a dream
Where everyone cared for each other,
I had a dream
Where there were no crooks,
I had a dream
Where everyone respected each other.

**April Green (11)**
St Francis Xavier School, Richmond

## I Have A Dream

Dream
That white people and black people were equal
Dream
That racism was wiped out
Dream
That all kids treated each other as they would like to be treated
Dream
That bullying was wiped out
Dream
That every country was fair to its people
Dream
That the world was a safe place for everyone to live
Dream
That the way we live now was made even better
Dream
About the future for your children.

**Devon Lowe (12)**
**St Francis Xavier School, Richmond**

## I Have A Dream

Dreams
Shooting stars
Some bad dreams
With monsters and devils
Things can happen to me
That can change everything
Dreams can be
Bad or
Good.

Imagine
The stars
Shining like glitter
And clouds, warm, fluffy
Friends, family here with me
Happiness in the air
Everyone here together
All here
Forever.

**Hayley Gill (12)**
**St Francis Xavier School, Richmond**

## I Have A Dream

I had a dream about you one night,

H aving fun and dancing in the moonlight,
A shooting star flickering around,
V ery quiet and no sound,
E verybody had a good night,

A ll the people then got a big fright,

D reams then make you weep,
R uining a good night's sleep,
E very time you have a dream
A nd whatever you do, do not be . . .
M ean!

**Lucy Bartram (12)**
**St Francis Xavier School, Richmond**

## I Have A Dream

The entire world wages war on each other,
We are full of pain,
Every day the world turns round,
Someone dies again.

There are two ways to exit this world
And the second should not be done,
It is murder, shot or diseases,
Why did they enter this Earth?
Beware in the streets, many carry a gun.

In the streets you are not safe,
You know not of who is there,
There are people who will hurt you,
These people do not care.

I believe that one day, the suffering will end,
The guns and murder shall be gone,
We will heal one day,
But where did we go wrong?

**Joe Mingay (12)**
**St Francis Xavier School, Richmond**

## I Have A Dream

I have a dream . . .
A white cloud falls upon the Earth,
Which flows with cool fresh air,
It takes all creatures, grown to birth,
Into a world of care.

Meanwhile the world we live in,
Becomes erased of pollution and hate,
The old world full of sin,
There dawns a newborn gate.

Beyond the gate is light and love,
No room for evil there,
The sky shines blue and bright above,
No sea nor land is bare.

The creatures come back through the gate,
Into the newborn land,
They love the life of love not hate
And all go hand in hand.

No matter what colour or race,
No matter what shape or size,
The people all get by with grace,
The limit is the skies.

So this is how the world should go,
That's how I think it's best,
I feel much better now you know,
A place of love and rest.

**Rachael Ditchburn (12)**
St Francis Xavier School, Richmond

## My Dream

My dream is to live a life of freedom
And to be free from a life,
Of hospitals and going under the knife,
I wish that I could be normal,
Like everyone mostly is
And not to suffer from
Cystic fibrosis.

It's painful, hurtful, annoying
And I hate it.

My life is a bore, I need a door,
To open to a new life.

**Danielle Falconer (12)**
St Francis Xavier School, Richmond

## My Dream

My lovely dream is to be a bird with long golden wings,
Soaring in the sky where my heart sings.

To fly overseas to warmer countries,
To see lovely shiny blue lakes and dark green palm trees.

I will splash my wings in the cold blue lake
And in the large green palm leaves, a nest I'll make.

To always be free is my dream and to live in a world
That is not make-believe!

**Lauren Perry (11)**
**St Francis Xavier School, Richmond**

## A Dream I Have

I cannot change the world alone,

H ave confidence in yourself,
A dore all things beautiful,
V isit ill and sick people,
E njoy every joyful moment

A nd have all the fun you can

D ream about how you can make a difference,
R escue sick animals,
E veryone is happy
A nd relax,
M y dream is to try and stop global warming.

**Natascha Carne (11)**
St Francis Xavier School, Richmond

## I Have A Dream

I could try and stop global warming,

H elp people on the streets,
A dore the world,
V isit sick people and give them presents,
E veryone is happy,

A dmire all the countryside and beauty of the world,

D edicate something in memory,
R elax and enjoy life,
E njoy the world and be happy forever,
A dore animals,
M ake the world a better place.

**Victoria Carter (12)**
St Francis Xavier School, Richmond

# I Have A Dream

I have a dream
    Of peace all over the world.

I have a dream
    To help my friends and family.

I have a dream
    To change the world,
    To help people speak their minds,
    To help stop poverty
    And racism.

I have a dream
    To help charities,
    And to be a good person.

I have a dream
    To be exact
    I have a lot.

**Hannah Hill (12)**
**St Francis Xavier School, Richmond**

## I Have A Dream

From the field to the desert,
From the mountain to the valley,
No weapons to be wielded,
Everyone would be happy.

'Food for everyone!'
The government will say,
There will be enough,
Day after day after day.

Everyone will be heard,
Everyone can speak,
Opinions are excellent,
Even if they're weak!

War is so foolish,
Let's make it stop,
Otherwise in this world,
Human population will drop.

**Jemma Elliott (13)**
**St Francis Xavier School, Richmond**

## World Poem

I have a dream,
That stars fill the sky,
I have a dream,
That poverty ceases,
I have a dream,
That global warming ends,
I have a dream,
That the world never ends,
I have a dream,
That words change the world,
I have a dream,
That we are making a difference,
I have a dream,
That you are the light in the dark,
I have a dream,
That you are inspiring others,
I have a dream,
That the world will live as one,
I have a dream.

**Jennifer Barker (13)**
**St Francis Xavier School, Richmond**

## I Have A Dream

I have a dream,
Where there's no grief or pain.

I have a dream,
Where there's only happiness and love.

I have a dream,
Where there's no fighting or killing.

I have a dream,
Where there's only peace and care.

I have a dream,
Where there's no criminals and bullies.

I have a dream,
Where there's only sharing and help.

I have a dream,
Where everyone tries to make their dreams come true,
So that is what I will do.

**Anna Regan (13)**
**St Francis Xavier School, Richmond**

# Dreams

I'm feeling tired now,
Ready to go to sleep,
My eyelids are heavy,
I am going to have a dream.

As I float into dreamworld,
I open up my eyes,
But what I see here is not a pretty sight.

Instead of pretty flowers
And birds flying high,
There is a frozen wasteland
And a dark midnight sky.

Underneath my feet it feels like ice,
I am freezing now, in the dead of night,
No one is here, as far as I can see,
Where is the light? Where is light?

Is this a nightmare, or am I actually asleep?
I am trying so hard to open up my eyes,
But the darkness just keeps closing in,
Suffocating me as I scream.

I am being dragged down,
To more unbearable darkness,
There's no going back . . .

**Sophie Carter (13)**
**St Francis Xavier School, Richmond**

# I Have A Dream - Words To Change The World

I have a dream,
Everyone has equal rights,
To love one another,
Stand up for what they believe,
Even if they are standing alone.

I have a dream,
For no one to live in poverty,
For everyone to have an education,
For everyone to eat and drink clean water
And live in a peaceful place.

I have a dream,
For wars to end,
Fighting to stop,
I have a dream,
For the world to be a better place!

**Frances Finn (13)**
**St Francis Xavier School, Richmond**

## I Have A Dream

I have a dream of a better place,
A place where everyone's equal,
No matter what race,
No matter what colour,
No matter what size or age.

Why does it matter where people are born?
Why does it matter where they live?
Why does it matter what colour they are?
Why does it matter what race?
It shouldn't in a land of grace.

**William Alderson (13)**
St Francis Xavier School, Richmond

## I Have A Dream

Words to change the world

I dream of a place,
Where hate is no more,
I dream of a place,
Where there is no war.

I dream of a place,
Where everyone is loved,
I dream of a place,
Where no one is mugged.

I dream of a place,
Where there is no sin,
I dream of a place,
Where anger's in the bin.

I dream of a place,
Where poverty has gone,
I dream of a place,
Where the murder rate is none.

I dream of a place,
Where this dream is true,
I dream of a place,
Where we can start anew.

**Danielle Cawood (13)**
**St Francis Xavier School, Richmond**

## Dreams

The world has a dream,
That there is no war,
No pain, no sorrow,
Just one law.

That everyone is equal,
Has the same rights,
Respects one another,
There are no fights.

Dreams can come true,
Just believe in yourself,
You can achieve anything,
You don't need wealth.

Follow your dream,
Live your life to the max,
Be careful, be happy,
Learn new facts.

**Hannah Robinson (13)**
**St Francis Xavier School, Richmond**

# I Have A Dream

I have a dream,
That's what they say,
To change the world,
On a future day.

Will it happen?
No one knows,
They'll just protest
And follow their nose.

So off they go,
Through war and court,
It's only a dream,
A dreamy thought.

They hope one day,
They'll stop things bad,
They dream that soon,
We'll never be sad.

We have a dream,
To help those folk,
Those hungry people,
Their hearts are broke.

We send the food
And things brand new,
Although they're dying,
It's all we can do.

Call me bad,
But I think it's mad,
The world's getting worse
And it's really sad.

I have a dream,
That's what they say,
To change the world,
On a future day.

**Paige Howard (12)**
**St Francis Xavier School, Richmond**

## I Have A Dream . . . Words To Change The World

I have a dream where people all get along,
No matter what colour or where we belong.

I have a dream where people are treated with respect,
Doesn't matter if we are not all perfect.

At the end of the day, we are part of God's creation,
Reading this poem, use your imagination . . .

If everybody could agree,
Would the prisoners of life be free?

**Lilly McNabb (13)**
St Francis Xavier School, Richmond

## I Have A Dream

I have a dream,
That one day England will win the World Cup again,
I have a dream,
That there will be no more war,
I have a dream,
To stop all the racism,
I have a dream,
To stop cutting trees down,
I have a dream,
For no more pollution,
I have a dream,
That there will be more snow,
I have a dream,
That will keep going on.

**Sam Thompson (13)**
St Francis Xavier School, Richmond

## I Have A Dream - Words To Change The World

I have a dream where we all live in peace,
Where war begins to cease,
Too many have already died,
To you I confide.

I have a dream where poverty is no more,
Where we can all walk through that open door,
Why are some people treated bad?
When I think about it, I feel so sad.

I have a dream where there is no discrimination,
Where people get along, across each nation,
We should treat everyone with respect,
Even if they are not perfect.

**Ryan Bishop (13)**
**St Francis Xavier School, Richmond**

## I Have A Dream

I have dreams,
Good dreams,
Bad dreams,
All sorts of dreams.

In my good dreams,
I imagine a world that is mine,
A perfect world,
A pretty world.

In my bad dreams,
I see the world that is my worst enemy's,
That person hates the world,
They destroy it.

But when I wake up,
I am back in the real world,
But never mind,
I just remember,
No dream is too small,
No dream is too big.

**Sophie Meehan (12)**
**St Francis Xavier School, Richmond**

# If Only I Could Be There!

I have a dream,
Galloping along the fields,
Jumping fences big and wide,
My brilliant pony clearing them all.

It all goes so quick,
I am nearly finished,
But it was really fun,
I wish I could start all over again.

Time to get off,
What a shame,
But he's been so good,
So I will wash him down.

It was a clear round straight,
Oh yes I am so proud,
My little pony - isn't he great,
He's going to get a lot of treats tonight!

But I've woken up and it's only a dream,
I wonder if next time it will really be true,
Why? I just wish I could be there,
Why won't it happen?

It's my destiny to do badminton,
If only I could be there,
I really wish I could!
But don't worry, you should see me there!

**Rebekah Slinger (12)**
**St Francis Xavier School, Richmond**

## If I Have A Dream

If I have a dream,
Peace would be
If I have a dream,
Harmony would be,
If I have a dream,
Children's rights would be made,
If I have a dream,
More laws would be made,
If I have a dream,
Peace would be,
If I have a dream,
Harmony would be,
If I have a dream,
Understanding would be easier,
If I have a dream,
People could understand me easier,
If I have a dream,
Peace would be,
If I have a dream,
Harmony would be.

**Stephanie Shepherd (12)**
**St Francis Xavier School, Richmond**

## I Had A Dream

I had a dream a long, long time ago
And still I wait for it to pass once more,
For when it comes I then will know,
That freedom will arise in us again.

And though we stand on brink of death and pain,
The lines of slaves and toil will not be broken,
For the children of our fathers will now say,
'Away with slavery in our land of Africa.'

Away with conflict and the cause of war,
Away with racism and injustice so cruel,
And give us hope that we may be a part,
A community of blacks and whites as one.

It came to me a long, long time ago,
As a wisp or memory of a passing dream,
That even I can change the paths of the future,
However small my rights and strengths may be.

When one day we stand collectively and proclaim,
Our right as people of the worldly nation,
It's unjust! It's unfair in our land of Africa,
Slaves we are and slaves until we're done.

I had a dream a long, long time ago
And still I wait for it to come again,
But shining through the conflict and the drama,
Are hopes of rainbow countries that prevail.

**Elizabeth Roe (12)**
**St Francis Xavier School, Richmond**

## I Have A Dream

Dream
For equality
For righteousness
For understanding
Dream
For a better future
For united countries
For no more poverty
Dream
For children with no fears
For children with bright futures
For acceptance
Dream
To make it reality.

**Kaitha Pennell (12)**
**St Francis Xavier School, Richmond**

## World At Peace

When peace shall come to this world,
People shall no longer kill,
No longer steal and no longer die.

People shall smile for the rest of eternity
And their smiles shall be seen all around the world.

The wars shall all finally end
And the armies will take care of peace.

People will look after people
And everyone will live for evermore.

**Ben Wilbor & Thomas Armstrong (12)**
**St Francis Xavier School, Richmond**

## I Had A Dream

I had a dream that everyone was nice,
I had a dream that there was no fighting,
I had a dream that there were no world wars,
I had a dream that there was peace and harmony,
All around the world.

I had a dream that there was no death!
I had a dream that everyone was faithful to each other,
I had a dream that there was no prison,
I had a dream that there was no poverty or starving.

I had a dream that there were no robbers,
I had a dream that there was no bullying,
I had a dream that there were no guns,
I had a dream . . .

I had a dream that the world had no weapons,
I had a dream that you would always have friends,
I had a dream that you could be nice to get what you want,
I had a dream, I had a dream.

**Matthew Atkins (12)**
**St Francis Xavier School, Richmond**

# I Have A Dream

I had a dream that everything was peaceful,
I had a dream that there was no war,
I had a dream that all races worked in harmony,
I had a dream . . .

I had a dream that no one was sad,
I had a dream that there was no wounded,
I had a dream that there was no blind,
I had a dream . . .

I had a dream that no one was deaf,
I had a dream that no one was blind,
I had a dream that no one could die,
I had a dream . . .

I had a dream that there were no robbers,
I had a dream that there was no bad,
I had a dream that there was no fight,
I had a dream . . .

I had a dream where there was no night,
I had a dream where there was no fright,
I had a dream where no one was only right,
I had a dream, I had that dream . . .

**James Walker (12)**
St Francis Xavier School, Richmond

## I Have A Dream

My dream!
If I had a dream
The world would be in peace
If I had a dream
I could have a wonderful space
If I had a dream
I could be a star in the sky
If I had a dream
We would be able to fly
If I had a dream
There would be no poverty
If I had a dream
There would be no one living on the streets
If I had a dream
No one would have to starve
If I had a dream no one would be killed
If I had a dream
This would all be true!

**Sophie Whittaker (12)**
**St Francis Xavier School, Richmond**

# I Have A Dream

We will have no more -

A world without war,
With no dead people on the floor,
Will open a door
And we will have no more war.

Either black or white,
We all have an equal right,
We shall share the same sight
And we will have no more racism.

We hear you crying
As if you're dying,
People are sighing
And we will have no more
Child abuse.

She's calling me names,
As if she's playing games,
It's always the same
And we will have no more
Bullying.

Everyone's the same,
Even though people call us names,
People are never too plain
And we will have no more,
Abuse or religion.

However different,
However the same,
We are all one big family,
Working together to get rid
Of all these things.

We will have no more . . .

**Emma Everitt & Chelsea Jones (13)**
St Francis Xavier School, Richmond

# War Rap

This is a rap about war,
Because we are sick of people being buried under the floor.

Because you kill them for no reason at all,
You reckon you're big and tall.

There is no difference between black and white,
So why do you need to make it a fight?

Because people get hurt for no reason at all,
You reckon you can stand there big and tall.

Everyone is different in their own way,
So there is no reason to pick on someone who's gay.

Because you call them names for no reason at all,
You reckon you are big and tall.

Because they are from a different race,
There's no reason for a court case.

Because you kill them for no reason at all,
You reckon you're big and tall.

This rap is to stop war,
So no one else is buried under the floor!

**Emma Snodgrass & Louise Pearson (13)**
St Francis Xavier School, Richmond

## I Have A Dream

I have a dream there will be no more war
And to prevent it they will make new laws
To ban all weapons made to hurt
That would be the best thing anyone saw.

I have a dream that people will unite
And not have hearts filled with spite
That the word racism will never be
And then we as people can reach new heights.

I have a dream that people feel safe
And no one is able to feel any hate
If you crash or injure someone
Or even if you're late.

**James Simpson (13)**
St Francis Xavier School, Richmond

## I Dream . . .

I dream there is no war,
No homework to make my hand sore,
Enough food held in the store
And a warm house when I walk in the door.

I dream of a world in peace,
With no need to call the police,
No criminals to release,
Just a world living in peace.

I dream there is no hate,
No one scared to go out late,
Even now there is no debate,
Why should people live in hate?

I dream of a world without any drugs,
No reason to go join the bugs,
Because of people who are thugs,
Another reason to stop drugs.

I know this is just a dream,
But if it were true,
Would the world still be so blue?

**Kate Renolds-Scott (13)**
**St Francis Xavier School, Richmond**

## Poem

The world is full of war,
People dying on the floor.

People are on drugs,
And there are horrible, nasty thugs.

Black or white, rich or poor,
We don't want to see any dead on the floor.

The guns keep popping
And people keep dropping.

Lots of discrimination,
Across the nation.

Please help it stop,
So the violence drops.

**Rhianna McCowan (13)**
St Francis Xavier School, Richmond

# I Have A Dream

The world is full of war,
People dying on the floor.

Begging them to stop,
But then the guns keep going pop!

More people dead,
Is it all in our head?

We want no more!

People have the same rights,
So there should be less fights.

Blacks, whites are the same,
Don't give them the blame.

We want no more!

**Louise Davies (13)**
**St Francis Xavier School, Richmond**

## I Have A Dream!

Before I sleep you are not there,
For all the time we share,
When together it feels so good,
Yet that is how it should.

This is a special world for you and me,
But only which I can see,
If I could have one wish,
It would be to wake up to a kiss.

We're back together, stronger than ever,
But you and me, no, never,
It's all visual and can't be true,
But I will never forget you.

I think to myself, *could this be true?*
*Am I really standing in front of you?*
This dream is nice, I don't want to be dead,
Too bad, it happens only when I'm in bed.

My dream of me and you!

**Abbie Taylor (14)**
**St Francis Xavier School, Richmond**

## I Have A Dream

How come there is so much difference in one world?
The line of destiny happens to be swirled,
Some people get good stories and some bad,
Some just accept it as the best life they've ever had.

Casey is a young girl, who lives a nice life,
One day she will make someone a lovely wife,
She has enough food and enough water,
One day she will have a beautiful daughter.

Tatamkula lives in a horrible place,
He often has dirt across his face,
Will he live until he's thirty?
It's because the water's dirty.

These two people are worlds apart,
So open your wallet and open your heart,
A little money can go a long way,
Let's all donate to charity today.

**Kerry-Ann Gray (14)**
**St Francis Xavier School, Richmond**

## I Had A Dream

I had a dream about me and you
We were so happy
And nothing could stop us two
We were friends forever.

We had so many good times
No one could change them ever!
They would always be with me and you
We were friends forever.

We had so many laughs
We had so much fun
I'll never forget the time you made me run!
We were friends forever!

We've been through some tough times
But we've made it through
The only one I ever trusted was you
We were friends forever.

So my dream was about me and you
We were so happy
And nothing could stop us two
We were friends forever.

**Rachael Baty (14)**
St Francis Xavier School, Richmond

## I Have A Dream . . .

We all have dreams
But what do they mean?

For peace?
For people?
Family or friends.

We all have dreams
But what do they mean?

No fights, friendship,
No hatred, happiness,
Smiles or laughter.

We all have dreams
But what do they mean?

For harmony?
For community?
Children or carers.

We all have dreams
But what do they mean?

No poverty, paradise
No racism, respect
Any country, any colour.

We all have dreams
But what do they mean?

For love?
For forgiveness?
Hate or crime.

We all have dreams
But what do they mean?

We can hope
We can wish
But will it come true?

**Katie Cunningham (14)**
**St Francis Xavier School, Richmond**

## I Have A Dream

Going to sleep was the best part of the day,
Being unleashed to a different land far away,
All I needed was a strong imagination
And I was the queen of my nation,
We'd sing and dance around the fire together,
I'd worn a great hat topped with a dodo feather,
I had my own spring pool and waterfall,
I could see from my tree house up high and tall,
All this is good but the truth is not at all,
I'm Katie from Catterick and cannot sing,
And I'm not the queen and far from the king!
The dodo's extinct and no feathers have been found,
And my pool is the fishpond in which I nearly drowned,
Overlooked by my semi detached house,
This is far from my dream home in a luxury tree house.
I may not have my great dream come true,
But I know I'm lucky to be equipped with a loo,
As there are many out there with nothing to live for,
No house, no food, their only bed is the floor,
So when we are in bed and wrapped up warm,
Sheltered away from the rain and the storms,
We should think of them and say a short prayer,
And find a good way to show that we care!

**Katie Brown (14)**
**St Francis Xavier School, Richmond**

## I Had A Dream

One night I had a dream,
That the world would be in peace,
That all the countries, towns and cities,
Would be in harmony.

One night I had a dream,
That we would accept each other,
That all the races, cultures and ages,
Would open their arms and welcome each other
And live as one in one.

One night I had a dream,
That everything would be safe and calm,
The birds would fly,
The rivers would flow,
All in unity.

One night I had a dream,
That there were no poor,
Everyone shared their money,
To stop the poverty,
Everyone was together.

One night I had a dream,
That if all of this was true,
If there was peace, and welcoming,
Safety and calmness,
The world would be a better place.

**Gareth Handley (12)**
**St Francis Xavier School, Richmond**

# I Have A Dream

I have a dream,
That everyone will
Look out their window sill
And never want anymore,
Than peace and no more war.

We are greedy now and have to just remember,
People are worse off than you,
So, when you throw your food away,
Think of the people starving day by day,
You may think you're really cool,
Wearing those flashy trainers to school,
I think people are cool,
When they pay for the poor to go to school.

We are grateful so we say,
That we get things day by day,
Some people are excited when they get food,
It puts them in a jubilant mood.

When you put food in the bin,
Think of the sin,
Now think of those when you pray,
Who walk to get water every day,
This is the world as it rotates today,
If aliens came down, what would they say?

**Paul Dury (12)**
**St Mary Redcliffe & Temple CE School, Bristol**

## Nightmare Storm

I was on a sailing ship, in the middle of a storm,
The ship was made of wood and iron, and its sails were
                                        ripped and torn,
I looked around the deck for people, but there was no one
                                          else on board,
When suddenly a pirate appeared wielding a sword.

I was scared: I tried to shout,
But when I opened my mouth no sound came out,

I wondered what would happen when he stabbed me with that sword,
The thunder howled, the lightning crashed, and
The rain it still poured.

'This is the end!' the pirate said, and I knew it too,
I knew that it was over, there was nothing left to do.

I was trying to scream, crying out for dear life,
It felt like being pierced by some horrible knife,
The darkness overtook me, and then I saw the light,
Literally! All I had done was sleep through the night!

**Gareth Bromley (12)**
**St Mary Redcliffe & Temple CE School, Bristol**

## I Have A Dream

I have a dream most every night,
It's like I'm looking out a broken window,
With a perfect frame and perfect pane,
But what's behind it is what really matters.

There is no racism,
No terrorism or sexism,
There are no fights
And friends are friends
And no one is pretend.

In my dream no one cries
And no one has depression,
There is laughter in the air,
Oh and everything is downright fair.

But when I wake up in the morning,
I see out of my cracked and shabby window
And I realise that none of it will stop,
As this world is truly selfish,
But my dream will never stop and we
Should try to make it happen,
That is my dream.

**Jessica Warrey (12)**
**St Mary Redcliffe & Temple CE School, Bristol**

## The Word Of A Dreamer

I am a dreamer,
Whenever I enter the world of deep slumber,
Dreams soar in my head like shooting stars,
Each waiting to be dreamt.

My dreams are strange,
They are all the same but they are all very different,
They are all infinite but they all only last for a moment
And they are simple, but they are all extremely complex.

Wild things happen in my dreams,
Pigs have wings and lollipop trees grow in clouds,
Holy tears fall from the sky, each with a different flavour
And bees do not sting, but release pure happiness.

My dreams are like puzzles,
They have hidden codes and inner meanings,
Locked under a chocolate key,
But the meaning I never understand.

Here is my story,
The story of a dreamer, who dreams strange dreams,
About pigs with wings, flying carpets
And scuba diving elephants.

My story is short!
But also very long, in a way nothing exists,
This world is not my own, not yours,
My only world exists in my dreams.

My life is cold,
'Tis so unfair that this life lives itself this way,
If I surely could, I would only ever dream,
Not having to live.

Hear my word,
For nothing can compare to the word of a dreamer.

**Amy Dutch (12)**
St Mary Redcliffe & Temple CE School, Bristol

# Dreams I Have . . .

There are many dreams I have,
Some I can achieve, and some I cannot have,
One of my dreams is playing for Arsenal FC
And becoming the next Thierry Henry,
Passing between each player, scoring free kicks
And giving the crowd a show with a few spectacular tricks.

Another of my dreams is a bit more business like,
Not so simple as riding a bike,
Owning a multinational company,
Filled with mountains of money,
Using that money to help the Earth,
Like giving African children a chance at birth.

**Chad Edwards (13)**
**St Mary Redcliffe & Temple CE School, Bristol**